THE STRUGGLE IS REAL

purpose in the pain

KEAGAN HAYDEN

the struggle is real

the struggle is real

The Struggle is Real—Copyright ©2022 by Keagan Hayden

Published by UNITED HOUSE Publishing

All rights reserved. No portion of this book may be reproduced or shared in any form—electronic, printed, photocopied, recording, or by any information storage and retrieval system, without prior written permission from the publisher. The use of short quotations is permitted.

Scripture quotations marked MSG are taken from THE MESSAGE, copyright © 1993, 2002, 2018 by Eugene H. Peterson.
Used by permission of NavPress. All rights reserved. Represented by Tyndale House Publishers, Inc.

Scriptures marked (ESV) are from The ESV® Bible (The Holy Bible, English Standard Version®), copyright © 2001 by Crossway, a publishing ministry of Good News Publishers.
Used by permission. All rights reserved.

ISBN: 978-1-952840-19-7

UNITED HOUSE Publishing
Waterford, Michigan
info@unitedhousepublishing.com
www.unitedhousepublishing.com

Interior design: Talitha McGuinness, talitha@unitedhousepublishing.com

Author photograph courtesy of Maeghann Smith of Maeggy Sue Photography

Printed in the United States of America

2022—First Edition

SPECIAL SALES
Most UNITED HOUSE books are available at special quantity discounts when purchased in bulk by corporations, organizations, and special-interest groups. For information, please e-mail orders@unitedhousepublishing.com.

the struggle is real

table of contents

introduction 9
part I: trial 11
  chapter 1: trial 15
  chapter 2: theology of suffering 25
part II: truth 37
  chapter 3: the truth about trials & sin 43
  chapter 4: the truth is...our character needs to be refined & purified 53
  chapter 5: the truth is...we must take responsibility 67
  chapter 6: the truth about trials & growth 79
  chapter 7: in order to grow - pruning & crushing 87
  chapter 8: in order to grow - practicing humility & perseverance 101
  chapter 9: when trials have their full effect 113
part III: triumph 123
  chapter 10: triumph surviving 129
  chapter 11: here for the fight 141
  chapter 12: thriving after the fight 147

bibliography 161
about the author 165

the struggle is real

For Jill Wyatt Marshall without whom this book wouldn't exist.
Thank you for calling God's purpose out of me.

the struggle is real

introduction

Struggle, suffering, trial...whatever name you give it, it still hurts. It's still hard. Sometimes, you'll feel like it will kill you, making it dang near impossible to survive, even if your trials aren't exactly what the rest of the world would call unbearable. Truthfully, not all of our trials merit the definition of suffering by the way we seem to create hierarchies, as if our holiness is determined by our suffering.

Yes, it's obvious we are suffering when we are crushed with an earth-shattering blow. But in those moments, when we experience those inconspicuous trials each day, the domino effect begins. When we finally realize we are in the midst of the suffering, we are already looking for a way out, looking for where things went wrong, and possibly even questioning God.

BUT GOD...But God is still in the middle of those desperate times. He is working in ways we cannot see because it's difficult, if not unfathomable, to understand that there is anything beyond our hurt. It's His job to walk with us through it. He is our guide in the darkness. Our trials reflect a purpose from a good, loving God who is working to make us look more like Him. It's for this reason, we cannot negate another's suffering even though it doesn't look like ours.

When we are in the middle of our struggles and we are

hurting, it's easy to feel unseen—not only by the world but by God. Trust me; I've been there. The good news is that regardless of what we feel, God sees us in the middle of our circumstances, no matter what they may be. While our God is holy, sovereign, and all-powerful, He is also personal, working to sanctify each of us individually.

Did you catch that?

Regardless of how you feel, the truth is: you are SEEN.

It's easy to find ourselves comparing our struggles to the struggles of others around us, and that serves us in no way. Our daily struggles and how we handle them are dependent on so many factors: the day, our experiences, our strengths, and our weaknesses. Our reactions often reflect this, but we have the power to change what feels crushing by pressing into the truth of the Word and a God who never changes.

Let us be cautious as we approach this, though. Just because we have God, just because we believe God, and just because we trust God to be who He is, does not mean we cannot sit with our grief. It does not mean we cannot recognize and wrestle with our suffering. We cannot gloss over our suffering and move straight to the idea that God is doing something in it. Even Jesus was ministered to in His suffering; He even questioned why God allowed His suffering. We are allowed to feel all these things and are even expected to do so in order that we may know our Father more intimately.

The goal is that we would learn to struggle well so we may be used not only where God chooses to use us, but in the way He chooses to use us.

part I: trial

"And when things start to happen,
don't worry. Don't stew.
Just go right along.
You'll start happening too."

the struggle is real

a note on trial

Maybe we read that word, "trial," and—as we cringe a bit—a clear picture of what that means flashes into our minds. For a lot of us, it's something in our lives that has been going on for what seems like months (at the very least), and is something we feel merits the gravity of such a word. If we can't call what we're walking through in the moment *suffering*, we level down to *trial*. From there, we level down to *struggle*, and then, we land at *difficulty*. Anything less just shouldn't weigh on us. Or, at least that's what we are conditioned to believe.

Listen, friend, we've diminished our own trials for far too long. If we're going through something hard, let's call it what it is: suffering. Or maybe you're more comfortable with trial. Or struggle. I know those sound like we're walking through nearly catastrophic life events, but that isn't necessarily the case. We have to stop diminishing the hard things.

Don't get me wrong. We've been conditioned by the world to do this. We recognize that losing a loved one or battling cancer is likely a more difficult thing than day-to-day work to pay the bills. It's because of this we tend to think we don't have the right to call the day-to-day things hard; we don't get to say the burden weighs so heavily on us at times that we can't make it through without leaning on Jesus. We fail to recognize we each carry our difficulties differently. And somewhere in the middle of that, we forget that each day, in the middle of the most joyful and most devastating seasons of our lives, we absolutely cannot do it without Jesus.

You see, the God we serve is the God of the not-so-hard and the hardest-thing-we've-ever-gone-through. Regardless of the way we carry our struggles, He still reigns over all of creation. We still need Him to walk with us through it all.

Hear me, please. Do not negate the hard. (There's a fine line between just sitting in misery and recognizing that life is hard, but we'll get to that.)

You have suffered and will suffer.
You have faced and will face trials.
You have struggled and will struggle.

You don't have to stay in those places, but regardless of where you are, *trial* is a word with which we're all too familiar. Let's stop being afraid of it.

chapter 1: trial

the struggle is real

chapter 1: trial

Tears streamed down my face as I sat in the parking lot of my doctor's office. I felt alone, even with my husband sitting just a few feet away. The call two weeks earlier had left me shaken; the results of my biopsy weighed heavily on my soul. My mother had thyroid nodules too; benign ones. But the tone of the nurse and the doctor wanting to see me—what could it mean?

I tried to gain the courage to open the door of the Suburban and go in, but tears still washed my face. I was staring down the barrel of an unknown diagnosis. Until now, I had done well to wear the mask of all things being fine, but I just knew it had to be my biggest fear—cancer.

Refusing to let me stay in yet unwarranted grief, my husband broke the teary silence. "Let's go in and find out what is going on. It's going to be okay." With a prayer, he opened the door, ushering me toward truth.

I sat, waiting on the doctor, recalling the cancer diagnosis my father received just months earlier. Granted, it was just an easily removed skin cancer, but still…my body was tense, rigid, nearly paralyzed. I sat frozen, pretending like my heart was not about to beat out of my chest as the doctor entered the sterile, cold room.

"The biopsy came back, and there is a 5% chance this nodule is cancerous."

To be honest, I was a bit taken aback. A 5% chance? The concerned tone of the nurse's phone call and refusal to tell me anything, the fear, the tears…all for 5%. While I battled feeling like I had been melodramatic in the parking lot, I asked, "So, what now?"

We scheduled my first ever surgery in which the nodule would be removed and sent to pathology for an immediate biopsy. If the biopsy came back cancerous, my entire thyroid would be removed, and I would come out of surgery without it.

I left the doctor's office that day with drama in my wake, but better off than when I arrived. At least now I had answers and a plan.

I immediately wondered what the point of all this was. What was God trying to teach me in this moment? Or, in any of the moments that followed?

I began to wrestle with thoughts of suicide.

I was wracked with guilt over past sins that made me question my salvation.

I constantly worried about having an overdrawn bank account.

I could not find a job. Overqualified. Under qualified. Good grief; I just wanted to work! I wanted to be able to pay my bills.

I struggled, unable to get pregnant. Was it my body? Was there something wrong with me or my husband? Was I not eating correctly? Did I exercise enough? I'd failed, right?

What got me most was simply realizing that I could not function on a daily basis without encountering some sort of attack.

For the better part of two years, it felt like I just could not catch a break.

I spent many nights longing for sleep, getting up each morning feeling crazy and tired. I cried at least as many tears as any girl on *The Bachelor*. I wondered why I was feeling this way, why I was going through all these things, why I could not catch the break I so desperately wanted.

After all, isn't a life in Christ supposed to be more happy than sad? Was I not supposed to have more triumph than tribulation? I reasoned with myself that I could be doing something wrong, or maybe I was being punished, or—as crazy as it sounded—God was trying to teach me and grow me. I went back and forth, settling on each option hundreds of times.

I found myself thinking with the mind of the Old Testament saints: these trials were a form of punishment, God's wrath. I completely neglected what it meant for a righteous person to suffer, only looking to my sin and shame rather than the righteousness God sought to grow in me. Sure, this could be God's discipline, but it could also be purposeful in my walk—a tool of growth. I had to let go of trying to understand what was happening and trust God in all His wisdom, conceding that I might not ever discover the real reason for these trials, big and small.

It became a battle to stop myself from spiraling in fear. I

mean, sure; I knew what was going on, but there were still so many unanswered questions and the unknown of what surgery would be like. Again, my husband pointed me toward the truth: I could not give the enemy victory by remaining paralyzed by fear.

It took immersing myself in the truth of God's Word to realize this was a promise in the life of a believer: struggle, trial, and hurt. Just because I had God on my side did not excuse me from struggle. In fact, the opposite was true; I was guaranteed trials. The Bible tells us to "not be surprised at the fiery trial when it comes upon you" (1 Peter 4:12, ESV). The key word that guarantees trials? "When." It's not a matter of *if* we will encounter them, but rather, it is a matter of *when*. I could not help but think that tended to be foreboding; a bit less than encouraging, really.

Triumph lay ahead of me, though. I awaited my first surgery, teetering between fear and faith.

Adrenaline coursed through my veins as I arrived at the hospital. Every move I made was tentative, and even lying in the hospital bed, I could not relax. It seemed like I was holding my breath as they wheeled me back to the ice-cold operating room where my tension turned to shivers.

My eyes cracked open in recovery, what seemed like five minutes later. I faced the clock that told the truth; it had been forty-five minutes. That wasn't long, so either this was really good or really bad. The more I woke up, the chattier I became.

"Did they tell you?" the recovery nurse asked, not indicating anything.

Because I'm so sweet, I thought, *Girlfriend, you've been with me. I've been knocked out. Do you seriously think they told me anything? You literally watched me wake up acting like a drunk monkey.* All I had the energy to actually utter was, "No."

To this day, I can't remember if the recovery nurse or a doctor delivered the news, but I do know this: I got to keep my thyroid, and it was now prettier with the non-cancerous growth removed. Relief flooded through me, relaxing my body and mind.

This, my friend, is the life of a believer: trial, truth, triumph. It's a cycle each and every day of going through the pit, rooting ourselves in truth, and growing in Christ. Sometimes, of course, the suffering is long. Our relief seems to evade us, and it is as if our trial will never end. Other times, the trial is fleeting. As believers in Jesus Christ, we face both versions of trials. They were promised to us in the first chapter of James where we are instructed to "count it all joy, my brothers, when you [we] meet trials of various kinds" (James 1:2, ESV). These trials are producing the work of God in us, sanctifying us to look more like Him each and every day.

Hold up. Wait a minute. Do you mean to tell me I am faced with a trial of some sort every single day? That sounds exhausting.

Yes. Each day, we are faced with trials, but because they are part of our every day, we tend not to notice them. Ranging from minor inconveniences to life-altering dramas, we have even gone so far as to discount them, not calling them what they are: trials. But we shouldn't discount these daily difficulties. While they may not always be life-changing, they are still drawing us closer to the heart of the Lord as we move through the trial cycle. In this, we must also avoid comparing our trials to those that belong to others because every trial has a goal to accomplish. Sure, the way we carry them may be different, but God uses our individual trials to shape us into the people He wants us to be so He may accomplish His will.

We have to quit moving through our lives trying to understand the mind of God and realize that "it is the glory of God to conceal things, but the glory of kings is to search things out" (Proverbs 25:2, ESV). It's not my job to understand all the things in the mind of God. As a matter of fact, He reserves the right to not give us all the details because He is God, and His main goal is to grow us into His image. He wants to draw us into a deeper trust relationship with Him, and in order to do that, He has to take us to a place where we quit thinking with our finite earthly understanding and search for His while desiring to see the world as He does. David, the author of most of the Psalms, recognized this as he started most of his psalms with questions and lament, but after sitting with God a while in prayer, he began to recognize who God is: trustworthy, faithful, steadfast, and loving. Looking at David, I am reminded I have to take God at His Word and trust that Isaiah 55:8-9 is true. His thoughts are so far above ours because He sees the entire picture, whereas we simply see a pixel, if that. God knows what He is doing, whether we understand it or not.

For my thoughts are not your thoughts, neither are your ways my ways, declares the LORD. For as the heavens are higher than the earth, so are my ways higher than your ways and my thoughts than your thoughts.
Isaiah 55:8-9, ESV

Thankfully, God begins to give us understanding in His Word, where we find the truth about trials. He put the guarantee for trials in writing for two reasons. First, He desires that we are not taken by surprise as it says in 1 Peter 4:12. We cannot allow the enemy to have that advantage, but when we walk around with defeat scrawled across our faces, it's as if we don't even have this strategic battle advantage. Not only that, but James tells us these trials have a purpose to produce steadfastness in us "that you [we] may be perfect and complete, lacking in nothing" (James 1:4, ESV).

Regardless of the reason for the trials we face or the severity of the trials, we can know that our suffering will "reveal areas of need, areas of weakness, and wrong attitudes that need to be removed." These trials, while temporary, will create a genuine, solid faith, as Peter explains in 1 Peter 1:6-7.

We must get familiar with the cycle of trials because one thing is clear: we will face trials. What they do to us—what we *allow* them to do to us—is our choice.

the struggle is real

chapter 2: theology of suffering

the struggle is real

chapter 2: theology of suffering

"Literally, I have nothing to say. I cannot write a book because I have no idea what I would write about." My friend kept pushing me. She kept making sure I knew she thought I should write a book because she believed I had something to say.

I laughed in her face. More than once.

She watched me trudge through trial after trial, seeing God do work in me that I had not realized yet, and she was not about to just let it lie. She knew I was in the midst of a relationship forged in fire, learning that God is who He says He is and that He is making me into who He says I am. She knew I was learning the best way He could teach me, and this was through trials. Some of which were to grow me and some of which were due to my own stupid choices.

As a trusted companion, I returned to her often, disclosing the raw details of what was happening in my life. She saw me in the depths, but she saw the joy growing to carry me out.

"Have I told you I think you should write a book?"

I again giggled and rolled my eyes, guarding the secret that I had begun to jot down ideas.

My daily parade of tears began to subside, but I still found myself in the midst of floods as I served as a shoulder to cry on for others. It seemed as though any time I would sit with friends, I'd hear a story of a broken heart, life not going exactly as planned, illnesses, and this overarching idea that nobody could catch a break. Questions flew. Where was God in all of this? Why is God doing this? What is my purpose? Why does God allow bad things to happen to good people? Why me? What have I done? Is God punishing me?

Overwhelmed and just crawling out of the rubble myself, I sat most often in silence, occasionally sharing what I thought I was learning. My words were limited, and the encouragement I offered was likely bleak, but I was still getting the answers myself.

As I began to pray and share these encounters with my friend, I again heard, "You know, I think you should write a book." This time, I met her with a hot, nearly angry question begging for the subject. All she did was smile and encourage a book.

That night, I could not shake the conversation. If she believed so much in me writing a book, why would she not tell me what she thought it should be about?

The next day, another friend entrusted me with stories of her battles. In the middle of that conversation, it was as though God flipped the switch.

"This. This is what people need to hear about," I thought, and my mind trailed off, wrapping itself in thoughts of what

theology of suffering

God had been teaching me about Himself for the better part of two years.

The thoughts I had begun to jot down earlier turned into a list that exploded. I scribbled scriptures next to each sentiment, realizing the truth that paved the path to triumph. I researched the scriptures to be sure I was not missing a thing that I needed to learn. As I dove deep, I discovered that because God loves us so deeply and passionately, He allows us to experience trials.

I was floored. Why would allowing suffering be a part of a deep love for us?

As I investigated, needing an anchor of hope, I stumbled upon Paul's words in Romans.

...But we rejoice in our sufferings, knowing that suffering produces endurance, and endurance produces character, and character produces hope, and hope does not put us to shame, because God's love has been poured into our hearts through the Holy Spirit who has been given to us.
Romans 5:3-5, ESV

Look how Paul goes further as he explains that the righteous may suffer in order to be reminded of their weakness and their need for a Savior: "But he said to me, 'My grace is sufficient for you, for my power is made perfect in weakness" (2 Corinthians 12:9, ESV).

In coffee shops, over dinner, or cuddled up on the cozy couch in the safety of my home, I sat with others in their deep hurt, their trials, and their suffering. I heard cries for help, for answers, for hope. I saw as I looked back, desperation for a truth that each one could cling to as though it were a life raft. While each trial came with its own identity, the truth I knew to be in the genetic makeup of trials showed itself: each trial serves to glorify God and grow us more into His image.

This was followed closely by another piece of the genetic makeup of trials, "whether or not we understand why we experience trials, we need to have no doubt that God still loves us and will not leave us. [While it is true that we] may never have an explanation of God's purposes [we] can be confident that those purposes do exist and they are perfect." Romans 8:28 explains God is working for the ultimate good of our souls. He is in hot pursuit of His children being made more like Him so the world would see Him more clearly.

I won't lie to you; I sat in a trance several nights, staring into the black of my bedroom feeling nothing but doubt. How could God be working *this* for my *good*? There was literally nothing good about it, at least not when I thought, with my earthly mind, of each new battle. How was I supposed to keep getting up each day while encountering a new battle or fighting an old foe? I had nothing left, and doubt was consuming me. Something had to give.

Fortunately, God is not only big enough to handle our doubts, but He is tender enough to meet us in them, no matter how deep the doubt goes. Our God is the strength we need to prevent doubt from building its home in our souls. How? We take Him at His Word. We must believe the God who meets us in our messes is the same God that met Job in his.

Then the Lord answered Job out of the whirlwind and said: "Who is this that darkens counsel by words without knowledge? Dress for action like a man; I will question

you, and you make it known to me. Where were you when I laid the foundation of the earth? Tell me, if you have understanding. Who determined its measurements – surely you know! Or who stretched the line upon it? On what were its bases sunk, or who laid its cornerstone, when the morning stars sang together and all the sons of God shouted for joy?"
Job 38:1-7, ESV

And that's just the beginning.

For two chapters in Job, God questions Job about his knowledge and understanding of the world. Ultimately, God reminds Job-and the rest of us-that He laid the foundations of the world, putting Job in his rightful place. Every time I read this, I am immediately a little girl listening to her daddy, ashamed that I even thought about sassing him. It reminds me that God is, in fact, big enough to handle the world; He's the One who created it!

In our suffering, we have to come to know the same hard-won truth Job acknowledged when he answered God saying, "'Behold, I am of small account; what shall I answer you?'" (Job 40:4, ESV). While God is working for our good to grow us, it's not ultimately about us. While He is a personal God, we should not take the trials He allows in our lives as a personal attack. It's not really all about us as we've been led to believe all these years. Ultimately, "[God] does work in the lives of those who suffer to bring them to a fuller knowledge of Himself and therefore to glorify Him."

Our theology of suffering is formed when we see clearly, in the trenches, that God's Word is nothing less than absolute truth refining us, guiding us, and disciplining us.

...BUT WHY?

There are several reasons we experience trials, all of which are in the business of removing all of the junk from our lives so we become more like Christ. It's tempting to believe that none of the reasons we experience suffering are our fault.

Let me be honest: sometimes our own irresponsible choices are the reasons we suffer. Yes, Beloved; sin is a cause of trial. The reason for this is science, really.

In high school physics, you learned Newton's Third Law of Motion, "For every action, there is an equal and opposite reaction." No doubt, we have each experienced this truth in our lives. Maybe we trip over a stone, fall, and break a wrist. The act of tripping causes our fall which meets us with the equal and opposite immovable sidewalk. Something has to give due to the nature of the immovable sidewalk, so the energy we carried results in a broken wrist.

The same is true for sin. For every action, there is a consequence. We tend to think something like, "Oh, it's just a little pride." But in our arrogance, we word vomit, declaring our greatness alongside everyone else's inferiority. This is met with the equal and opposite reaction of the loss of a friendship or even hurtful comments about *us*. You see, even the smallest action has an equal and opposite reaction. There is no room for sin in perfection, so we earn death.

Unlike Newton's Law of Motion, our sin has a caveat: grace. We don't get an equal measure of consequence for our sin. If we did, we would be condemned to hell for eternity, BUT GOD sent His Son to take our place, to receive the full wrath of God so we might have eternal life. That does not free us from consequence, but it does free us from our absolutely deserved punishment: an eternity in hell.

Our choices, even the smallest of our sins, still carry consequences, even though our ultimate debt has been paid. Just like a broken wrist will still need to heal, the damage from our sin still needs repaired.

There are times, though, when God allows trials into our lives as a way to test us. This test is not a pass or fail sort of test. Instead, this is the type of testing that proves and strengthens us, purifying our motives for worshiping God (Romans 5, James 1:2-6, 2 Corinthians 1:5-7). Do not be deceived by thinking God is trying to entrap us or catch us red-handed; He already knows our sin, and tempting us is contrary to His very nature. Instead, He is allowing us to experience these temptations for our good. God's priority is that we look more like Him, evidenced by the fruits we bear.

It is also true that we will experience persecution as a result of being children of God, which might result in our suffering (2 Timothy 3:12). While this feels like injustice, we can take heart in the fact that we do not experience suffering alone; we have a brotherhood around the world that is suffering similarly. Christ Himself also suffered persecution (1 Peter 5:9, 4:13; John 15:20).

While there are various reasons for our trials, God allows them. Nothing happens on this earth that God is not privy to.

the devil works hard
Here's the deal, friend: while the enemy is undoubtedly real and at work, we as believers tend to hand power over to him that he does not deserve. We neglect to put on our armor,

we allow him footholds to wreak havoc in our lives, and we even think he has power over us to control our thoughts. I know that sounds dramatic, but it is true.

Let me tell you a secret the enemy does not want us to know.

While our adversary wants us to believe that he is for us, that he is on our side, he is, in fact, not on our side. He will tell us lies—yes, friend; that is what they are—that lead us to believe he is fighting for us when the reality is that he is actively fighting against us. He does not want to see us live our lives in victory because that means he loses. He enjoys causing pain and suffering.

Make no mistake. The devil and his posse of hateful demons are waiting to take advantage of the vulnerable, actively trying to tell us lies that sound like truths, to lead us away from the Truth. He is waiting to steal from, kill, and destroy us at the first opportunity.

The good news, though, is that Satan is still under the authority of God Almighty. He can only do the work God allows. We see this explained in Job 1:8-12 when God protected Job but chose to remove His protection, giving the enemy permission to afflict Job. And while it is true that Satan is actively working against us, God is always working for our good. Using any tactic he can come up with, the enemy thinks he can destroy us, but God can reverse it. He takes all things and makes them beneficial, even if it takes a while as it did for Joseph. While Joseph endured being sold into slavery, being wrongly accused, and thrown in prison, seemingly forgotten, he remained faithful to God, knowing this was all bigger than anything he could see. Joseph ended up being placed in a position of power when he came out of prison. His job was to help keep food reserves full for the nation. Despite the evil his brothers tried to inflict, many years later, Joseph recognized them when they came for food during a famine and showed them compassion. God used this evil for good (Genesis 50:20). The enemy may have gotten short-term victories, but ultimately, he failed.

I love the way it's described when Jesus says, "'It was not that this man sinned, or his parents, but that the works of God might be displayed in him'" (John 9:3, ESV). While Joseph got to see God work things for good, we may not get that chance. However, we must know that all our trials serve to glorify God. Our suffering has a purpose.

the struggle is real

part II: truth

"I'm sorry to say so
but, sadly, it's true
that Bang-ups
and Hang-ups
can happen to you.

You can get all hung up
in a prickle-ly perch.
And your gang will fly on.
You'll be left in a Lurch.

You'll come down from the Lurch
with an unpleasant bump.
And the chance are, then,
that you'll be in a Slump.

And when you're in a Slump,
you're not in for much fun.
Un-slumping yourself
is not easily done."

the struggle is real

a note on sanctification

If we are going to navigate our way through the purpose of trials through the lens of truth so that lies stand no chance, I want to be clear.

The process of us becoming more like Christ—a clearer reflection of Him—is sanctification. This can be anything that makes us more like Christ, ranging from cutting away the sins in our lives to growing by producing not only more fruit of the Spirit, but better fruit.

As Christians, we are no longer ruled by sin. Rather, we are slaves to righteousness, as Paul writes in Romans 6. We are now saved by grace.

So you also must consider yourselves dead to sin and alive to God in Christ Jesus. Let not sin therefore reign in your mortal body, to make you obey its passions. Do not present your members to sin as instruments for unrighteousness, but present yourselves to God as those who have been brought from death to life, and your members to God as instruments for righteousness.
Romans 6:11-13, ESV

As we continue in Romans 6, it becomes clear that as we

progress through our Christian lives, we are also progressing in becoming more like Christ.

Theologian Wayne Grudem postulates in his comprehensive book of doctrinal and theological explanations called Systematic Theology that, as believers, we have both an active and passive role in our walk with God. Our passive role is that we depend on God to do the sanctifying. Our active role demands that we not become lazy, as if we have no part in our becoming more like Christ. We must actively strive to obey God and take steps to seek out increasing sanctification.

Let us be careful to avoid assuming we can sanctify ourselves. The role of God in our sanctification is far greater than ours. He sanctifies us completely, according to 1Thessalonians 5:23.

Each person of the Trinity is at work in our sanctification:

Like any good father, God the Father takes on the role of disciplining His children. This is explained to us in Hebrews 12:5-11 as an act of immense love, as well as an honor bestowed upon us as children of God. We have all the rights as heirs, including the discipline of our heavenly Father.

God the Son took our place on the cross, bearing the full wrath of God, and ultimately earning our sanctification and setting the example of obedience. In this, we are able to see the discipline of God and His unfathomable love for us. He sees us in our sins and loves us, but He refuses to leave us there.

And God the Holy Spirit, so often overlooked because of His

constant work in our lives, does just that. He works in us to change our hearts and sanctify us.

When we feel like we do not have it all figured out or that we might not measure up to the standards of righteousness we have set for ourselves, it is important to remember that sanctification is not just about what we bring. We cannot sanctify ourselves. It is a cooperative effort between God and man. We are continually allowed to experience more freedom from sin and to more clearly reflect Christ in our lives.

We will never be able to achieve perfection. We can't. Sanctification is a lifelong process that will not be completed this side of heaven. We must simply keep pressing on and pressing into righteousness.

the struggle is real

chapter 3: the truth about trials & sin

the struggle is real

chapter 3: the truth about trials & sin

I stopped watching the nightly news a long time ago, and I usually end up having to ground myself from social media when the world seems to go off the rails. It gets to be too much.

I get overwhelmed.

I get sad.

I get angry.

I get hopeless.

I get hateful.

I find myself spiraling into toxicity where I become sucked into being part of the problem. I start spewing "facts" that I've only seen in headlines, and I limit my reading to what fits only my narrative of knowledge.

I begin to refuse to create a space for seeing police brutality take yet another life and witnessing the cries for help that manifest themselves in riots and what seems like complaints. I would rather stay ignorant. I refuse to even listen to both sides of the story when it comes to hot button issues; I've made up my mind, and my decision is final. I would rather not hear about yet another tragedy across the world because it seems like that is all we hear about, and quite frankly, it seems like we just cannot do anything about it. It's easier that way...

This putting up of my defenses so quickly and mercilessly is a reflection of the deep-seated problem of apathy and exhaustion that is a byproduct of a broken and fallen world.

Of course, we flip on the nightly news to images of riots and a long list of local, national, and global tragedies because we have long allowed darkness to reign. A broken and fallen world is not an excuse. Instead, it is a motivator to break the cycle, to pursue righteousness rather than sin.

However, in order to do that, we must put the trials we experience due to sin in their rightful place so the enemy has no hold. We must hold fast to truth when we are in the midst of trials resulting from the sin that plagues us.

You see, in the beginning, God created the heavens and the earth, and it was good. There was no sin. There was no evil. It was just His good, beautiful, profound creation, which He designed to bring Him pleasure and glory. He created man and woman to care for His creation, giving them dominion to rule over it. He entrusted them with a massive and beautiful gift, but He had one rule.

As they enjoyed their lives without shame, without need or want, but rather with peace, they experienced a deep, rooted, and personal connection with the Father. Unfortunately, the crafty serpent made an appearance and twisted the words of

God, putting seeds of doubt in their minds.

Despite the deep, personal connection with the Father, they fell for the lie of the enemy, and what did it get them?

While "God had given the natural world to them for their physical and spiritual well-being…that world now became a cause of suffering…It is, therefore, true to say that there is suffering in this world because there is sin in the world." We see this represented in Genesis 3:14-19 when it outlines the curse, which was the punishment for disobedience. No one escaped the curse. The serpent was sentenced to slither for all of time, with a promise of enmity between him and humankind. The woman was cursed with pain in childbearing, while the man was cursed to work and struggle for survival. This act of disobedience, the fall, earned us a life full of trials. While it would have been easier for God to simply look the other way, it would not have been loving.

His goal has always been to pursue us and make us the best thing we can be: a reflection of Him. Conversely, the enemy's goal is always to bring about our worst and turn us away from God. Because of that, our Father chooses to give us consequences for our actions so we may learn that these sinful decisions lead to destruction.

Unlike Satan, God does not take pleasure in causing suffering, but He is sure to discipline those He loves as sons and daughters. There has to be consequences for our actions; a payment for our transgressions. That is why "for our sake He made him to be sin who knew no sin, so that in him we might become the righteousness of God" (2 Corinthians 5:21, ESV).

In the Old Testament, the Hebrews often interpreted suffering as punishment and God's wrath for sin in their lives. However, suffering in the lives of the righteous posed a problem: why would God allow the righteous to suffer?

Trent Butler postulates three reasons the righteous suffer:
- God needs to get our attention.
- Our sin needs to be corrected into obedience.
- Our character needs to be refined.

While these are three good reasons to explain why we might suffer, we may never actually be able to figure out which one applies to the specific moment, and it is often a fruitless task to force meaning upon things only God is meant to understand. Similarly, we must trust God enough to know that He knows what He's doing, even if we don't get the understanding or closure we may so desperately desire. God gets it. He's big enough to handle our questions and our anger about trials. He knows we won't always understand—if ever—but it's a call to lean into Him and trust Him for our sanctification.

God needs to get our attention
When we were in college, my husband was a Sports and Exercise Science major, and I spent my time with the Fine Arts and Education departments as a Communication Studies major. We lived in two very different worlds, and we shared our stories from class with each other.

It seemed as though in each class, my husband had a female classmate who gravitated toward him. He would share stories about what they said or did in relation to the class and how that led to other conversations. At least once each semester, I would tell him, "I'm pretty sure that girl has a crush on you."

He always insisted the classmate most certainly did not have a crush on him. And, y'all, he truly believed it. He was completely oblivious to the more than obvious flirting. These girls could not seem to get his attention, no matter what they tried. (Good news for me, though!)

He, like most men, does not handle subtlety well, but these flirtations were not cases where subtly was employed. More often than we would like to admit, sometimes we miss the most incredibly obvious things.

When we look back at Job, we find one of his friends basically rebuking him. He's the friend we all need to keep us in check, telling Job, "Man, wake up! God has been trying to tell you something, to get your attention, and you are missing it, knucklehead!" (Job 33:14, personal paraphrase).

This friend of Job's was not like others. He supposed that God was at work and that He was doing something humans did not understand. It wasn't all about the punishment of sins, but God was possibly drawing Job to Himself in the midst of all these things. God was trying to get Job's attention. Unfortunately, like most of us, he missed all the previous messages God was trying to communicate, contrary to the lack of subtlety. One might even venture to say Job was thick-headed.

The truth is, when God needs us to pay attention and we are not, He has to take more drastic measures. He cares enough about us to not let us miss the important things He wants to teach us, whether it be ridding us of our sin or growing us to look more like Him. He doesn't want us to miss Him, and in today's fast-paced, self-consumed society, it's easy to overlook what God is trying to say to us. There's too much noise drowning out what really matters, making it a fight to keep God and the pursuit of His righteousness at the forefront of our minds.

God is wise enough to know that when we come under fire, we listen. We suddenly realize we are not enough to do this on our own, so He allows the fire. Job's friend continues to praise God's ways when he says, "He delivers the afflicted by their affliction and opens their ear by adversity" (Job 36:15, ESV). Truly, it may take the worst situation to give us the best, to teach us who we are supposed to be, and to show us who God is. When we are desperate, we will pay attention because nothing else matters. God uses even desperation to sanctify us.

our sin needs to be corrected to obedience
The key to creating good humans is discipline. We must be taught to obey because we have a sinful nature that does not create a bend toward obedience in us. Instead, we have a natural bend toward rebellion and sinfulness.

As my daughter grows into a tiny human, exercising her own independence, I must teach her what is right and wrong. I must teach her that when her daddy and I say something, she needs to listen. When my daughter chooses not to obey, there are consequences geared toward creating a habit of obedience.

God operates in the same way. After all, we had to learn the importance of discipline from somewhere too.

When we sin by disobeying God's commands (whether intentionally or not), we are faced with the consequences that correct our rebellion into obedience. This is so we honor and glorify God with our lives, making it evident we are no longer slaves to sin (as Paul says) but instead, slaves to righteousness. When we become Christians, we are new creations who are no longer bound by sin (2 Corinthians 5:17, ESV).

Unfortunately, as much as we try, we are always pulled by sin. When I correct my daughter and she finally starts to understand she must obey in one area, another area of disobedience rears its head, thus starting the cycle over again. Once we've mastered the obedience to not pull dishes out of the cabinet, we move to learning not to throw fits when we don't get our way. In the same way, God is constantly pulling the junk out of our lives as if plucking weeds from our souls each spring.

Peter does a great job of explaining this in the letter he writes to Christians scattered throughout the region in which he ministered.

"As obedient children, do not be conformed to the passions of your former ignorance, but as he who called you is holy, you also be holy in all your conduct, since it is written, 'You shall be holy, for I am holy.'... Having purified your souls by your obedience to the truth for a sincere brotherly love, love one another earnestly from a pure heart, since you have been born again, not of perishable seed, but of imperishable, through the living and abiding word of God; for 'All flesh is like grass and all its glory like the flower of grass. The grass withers, and the flower falls, but the word of the Lord remains forever.'"
1 Peter 1:14-16, 22-25, ESV

Peter camps out on the idea of obedience here, as he is talking about the holiness of the Christians. Interesting; isn't it? Our obedience is directly tied to being children of God. It's part of His work in us, serving as evidence to the lost world that we are being transformed. If we behave in a way that reflects disobedience, we reflect who we were before Christ. He continues on to encourage the believers to be holy, set apart, just as Christ is.

It would be easier if we were immediately inclined to obey, to perfectly "get it right." I hate when I mess up any little bit. As a matter of fact, some might say I'm a perfectionist. I don't do things halfway because if it's worth doing, it's worth doing right. I want to do things with a level of excellence. I want to be sure that what I produce is quality. Sometimes, this perfectionist attitude transforms me into a control freak, and I will do almost anything I can to make things happen the "right" way.

That's short-sighted, though. Often, I end up sacrificing excellence, or even worse, I end up driving myself crazy trying to pursue perfection. Perfection has become an idol, and to be honest, it has stripped me from resting in the truth that God saved me while I was still a sinner (Romans 5:8). He never expected us to come to Him cleaned up and perfect; He expects us to come to Him raw and ready for Him to work in us and through us. In other words, we act in obedience because Christ did, and we are to imitate Christ. This reflects a desire and pursuit of righteousness as the fruits of the Spirit are ever-increasing in us. The work done in us to make us obedient to Christ is an eternal work that is continually being done as we live and breathe. Our obedience is formed as we grow with Christ; it's not a simple switch that flips when we become followers of Him.

chapter 4: the truth is...
our character needs to be refined & purified

the struggle is real

chapter 4: the truth is...our character needs to be refined & purified

When God saves us, He wants us to reflect Him to the world. It should become our goal to imitate Him so others may know Him.

That is to say, we should strive for perfection since He went to the cross without sin. Blameless. Perfect. We are commanded to be "perfect as our Heavenly Father is perfect" (Matthew 5:48, ESV). But how do we do this, as we know from the rest of the Word, we will never attain perfection on this side of heaven? We will be plagued with the thorn that is sin, being sanctified until we reach Home.

Wayne Grudem puts it like this:
"When Jesus commands us to be perfect as our heavenly Father is perfect, this simply shows God's own absolute moral purity is the standard toward which we are to aim and the stand for which God holds us accountable. The fact we are unable to attain that standard does not mean it will be lowered; rather it means we need God's grace and forgiveness to overcome our remaining sin..."

God is not okay with simply leaving us in our sin. If He was, there would be no reason for a Savior, no need for atonement of sins, and no need for a perfect sacrifice. He sent His Son because He refuses to leave us in our sin. He loved us enough to pay the price, satisfying His own wrath so we might have eternal life! While the death and resurrection of Christ was the defeat of sin and death, putting the enemy on notice that his time to steal, kill, and destroy is limited, sin has not yet been eradicated. We are constantly fighting our flesh and striving for perfection we will never attain until we are in glory.

The Bible does a great job explaining this in Malachi 3:2-3, when we are told we will be purified as though by the fuller's soap and refined like gold and silver. While that's a beautiful picture of the care and time the process of purifying or refining takes, we often miss the point. The purifying by the fuller's soap and the refining by fire are processes that are both thorough and severe.

When washed with the fuller's soap, clothes are first washed with lye soap and then placed on rocks and beaten with sticks to remove all the impurities they may have picked up. And the refiner's fire? The heat has to be so intense that it melts gold and silver, bringing the dross (impurities) up to be separated from the purity of the metals. Both are intense processes of cleansing, yet profitable. Precious metals like gold and silver constantly undergo a process of becoming more pure. It's not a coincidence God is in the business of doing the same for us.

Unfortunately, we often spit hatefulness, idolize legalism, and pursue our own righteousness, all while attaching His name to these un-Christlike actions. Our interpretations of who Jesus is and what He does in us and for us are steeped in our own agendas, as we pick out Scriptures like trail mix.

We weaponize Scripture when it is used out of context.

We weaponize Jesus when we put His name on hate.

We weaponize righteousness when we claim our own agendas are morally right.

Hateful, legalistic, and self-righteous do not reflect a God anyone wants. That's not a God who is loving, savior of the vilest of sinners, or a God who is a life-changer. Simply, that's not the God of the Bible. Since that's not who God is, we can no longer stand for sinful pursuits once we are in Christ. In order for us to become like Christ, our character has to be refined.

While we will never be perfect on this side of heaven, we are to strive for the perfection of our Heavenly Father. It's a strange thing to be a human, existing in the tension of working towards perfection and not being able to achieve perfection.. It's in the in-between we see Jesus most clearly. He is both loving and just. Both truthful and merciful. Both compassionate and repulsed by sin. We have to strive for Christ-like perfection and rest in His grace. As Paul says, grace is not an excuse to keep on sinning. We are forgiven but held accountable. Our account debt was paid for on the cross by Christ, but that is not an excuse to live like Hell and claim Heaven.

As we strive to avoid sinning, some of our refinement comes through turning sin into obedience, and other parts of our refinement come because our sin is exposed. Our selfishness, hatefulness, pride, discontentment, legalism, traditionalism, idols, and other such things can no longer hide in the dark corners of our souls when the light of God shines on them. These sins no longer have a place to hide, so we must deal with them.

the struggle is real

It's a hard and painful process to confront our sin, and it often makes us uncomfortable. However, we must recognize there are consequences for our actions that fall short of perfection.

Because of our sin, we deserve Hell. The Bible tells us, "For the wages of sin is death, but the free gift of God is eternal life through Christ Jesus our Lord" (Romans 6:23, ESV). Hell is death made permanent, and that is what we earned the moment we began to sin. But God took care of that consequence for us, and He placed on His children righteousness instead.

The fact that we have been freed from the eternal wrath of God does not mean we are free from the task of earthly sanctification, where we work out our salvation and figure out what it means to follow Jesus. We are still subject to discipline when we mess up and when we sin. As a matter of fact, because God is a good Father, He must discipline us as any good father does.

We can no longer claim ignorance because of all the Holy Spirit teaches us. Instead, we must apply this insight to our lives, not turning a blind eye, but making the necessary changes to do better and be better—to live transformed lives.

The thing is, though, our sin does not affect just us. How selfish of us to think this. That's the heart of sin: an attitude of I.

I am the only one this affects, so why does it matter if I do it.
I am the only one who has to pay for this mistake.
I can do what I want. I won't hurt anyone else.

Oh, sweet friend, how wrong we are to assume our sin

only affects us. Sin wants to take captive as many as it can, knowing its time is short because death has already been defeated. Don't believe me?

Cain and Abel, the children of Adam and Eve, are the perfect example. Cain, jealous of his brother Abel who found favor with God due to a righteous heart, was angry. He nursed bitterness, resentment, and animosity toward his younger brother even after God Himself approached him with a challenge to turn his heart toward God and to do better. However, Cain chose to let sin reign, ultimately killing his brother. Not only did Cain's actions bring forth punishment for him, but those same actions cost Abel his life and cost Adam and Eve their second son. The grief that would assuredly accost these parents was not taken into consideration when the murder was committed, and it is likely the consequences for Cain himself were not considered. By way of his impulsive and sinful actions, Cain neglected to see the long-term effects or consider the cost: four people's lives forever changed.

But this sinfulness is a problem that plagues the entire timeline of the world. Years after Cain, King David looked upon Bathsheba and ultimately slept with her. In order to satisfy his selfish desires, he did not consider her husband who was away at war, that she did not want to sleep with him, or the guilt she might carry after the fact. As if that wasn't enough, David got Bathsheba pregnant and brought her husband home to make it look as though he was the father. This didn't work though because he was loyal to his troops and would not sleep with Bathsheba. Then, David sent the husband back to the frontlines of war and pulled back the other troops to leave him for dead. These actions affected more people than we can count as we consider the guilt Bathsheba had to carry from the affair with the king, coping with the trauma of being raped, the grief of losing her husband, the unborn child, and decisions as to how she might raise that baby. Not to mention, David had to deal with the consequences that affected him: the blood of Bathsheba's husband on his hands, an unplanned child, the guilt and shame of disobeying God, a loss of respect from his troops, and the list goes on.

Even the tiniest sin calls our character into question and exposes our need for refinement. King David committed a sin with extensive and obvious consequences, reminding us that the consequences of our sin extend further than we may ever know and might likely cause another's trials. Our sin is not exclusive to just us…it's a far-reaching cancer that impacts those around us as well.

Our sin does not ask us to look beyond ourselves, beyond our comfort, or beyond the status quo. Only God does that. When God refines our character, we cannot help but look beyond ourselves, while staring the outside of our comfort zone straight in the face.

The consequences we face cannot be escaped because we serve a righteous and just God. He will hold us accountable.

That's why He sent His Son.

There was the debt we owed and could not pay, no matter how long and hard we worked to pay it. God's wrath would never be satisfied without a perfect, atoning sacrifice. In His great love, grace, and mercy, He sent His Son to be that for us.

If the sacrifice of His only Son doesn't demonstrate the fact that God and sin cannot coexist, I don't know what does. Because of that, though, we are new creations who are no longer ruled by the flesh. There is a definite moral change in us at the point of our salvation. According to Titus 3:5, we experience a complete renewal of our souls at the point of regeneration, and because of that renewal, we cannot continue to live lives of sin. It's impossible.

We are not perfect, and we will never be in this lifetime. That fact does not excuse us from continually being purified. God is in the business of making us perfect and complete, so He cannot leave us as we are.

In order to sanctify us, He allows trials to assail us, even—and maybe especially—when we bring them on by our own choices. These trials expose our need for a Savior more than anything in this world.

When I was seven, I knew I needed a Savior, but my senior year of high school I seemed to forget whose I was. I began living for myself, and because of it, I hated that year. I was seventeen, ready to take on the world. Yes, I knew I was a Christian, but I surrendered to myself rather than God.

The air was still warm outside with just a hint of crispness as fall approached. Senior year started well. I was adjusting to my new college level classes, an off-period, and a new boyfriend: a sophomore who said he was a Christian. He captured my attention, and that was good enough.

In the first few weeks of us dating, I had a bit of an uneasiness in my spirit. This uneasiness only increased as I learned of his bout with alcohol poisoning over the summer and heard some of the conversations that came out of his mouth. While these were small things, they didn't sit well with me, and I didn't want to spend much time with him. On the other hand, I didn't really want to break up with him because I felt I had a boyfriend who was good to me, and I thought I was in control. I liked the idea of being in control and thought I could simply limit interactions but maintain the relationship. After all, I was just in high school; how serious did this need to be, anyway?

By about month two of our relationship, it became apparent he wanted to take things further physically, and that was not a line I was willing to cross. I stood my ground, and it seemed like he understood. Not a week later, I found myself in a position I never thought I would be in. While we never had sex, I can honestly say I did not stand my ground.

Our relationship lasted the duration of my senior year. All the while, I kept finding myself pursuing fleshly desires rather than God's plans. I kept caving to physical pressures because I didn't want to lose this boyfriend (To this day, I still can't tell you why except that I thrived on the illusion I was in control).

Early in the summer, just after graduation, I went to a Christian leadership camp. At this camp, I knew, without a shadow of a doubt, God was asking me to break up with this boy. I had the bright idea to text him and let him know we would be talking when I got back. He was smart enough to know what that meant, so he pulled me into a conversation. It was at that point I chose him over God.

We dated for another month. All the while, I was miserable. I felt a broken relationship with God like I was no longer a

Christian because of this. When I finally got the courage to actually break up with him, those feelings remained, but I was good at pushing them aside.

I kept doing the work. I was involved in our college ministry, served as a summer intern at the church, led mission trips, and desired to be right in the center of God's will. It wasn't until I had been married three years that I was forced to deal with the consequences of the relationship from my senior year. It was time for healing, for freedom, and for the real work to begin. I could no longer keep putting a band-aid over this wound, but I didn't realize yet that healing wounds meant allowing them to be exposed so the Healer can properly clean, medicate, and dress them.

I sat on my bedroom floor blow drying my hair, just staring into space when suddenly the word "suicide" popped in my head. I was taken aback because nothing in my world was related to that at the moment. I continued to blow dry my hair, trying to figure out what was going on, but I ultimately blew it off.

Unfortunately, the thought kept recurring. Just a word, but enough to startle me. I never had suicidal thoughts. I was never depressed. I never…What was this?

This was a surfacing of the enemy after I gave him a foothold all those years ago. This was an attack. This was doubt. This was guilt. This was war.

I began a two-year-long process of having to deal with guilt and shame from those mistakes—weeding out the lies of the enemy. This trial saw me through purification by truth.

Through conversations with my husband and immersing myself in the Word, I was forced to relearn the truth that even when I mess up, God still pursues me and uses my junk for Him. He uses the fact that we need a Savior to teach us more of His love, His character, and His grace. God did not leave me in my guilt, shame, and depression. Instead, He removed it, as all of it was exposed to the light. He remained faithful to me even when I was in the midst of running. That's who He is. I still had to make the choice, though: Did I want to remain depressed, guilty, and shameful, or did I want to "press on toward the goal for the prize of the upward call of God in Christ Jesus" (Philippians 3:14, ESV).

It is not easy to let God purify, refine, and chisel away all the junk that doesn't belong, but it is well worth it. If it were up to the old me (me before Christ), I would have chosen to remain in the dark. It seemed safer there, and while it may not have been fulfilling, it was comfortable.

The thing about God is, He isn't really interested in our comfort. Instead, He is interested in being our Comforter: our enough. When we experience salvation, we are brought into the family of God. We were chosen as His, and as such, we inherit all the rights that come with being a member of His family, including His love and His discipline. Because of this, we have to reorient our desires toward righteousness so we might not be bound to the sin and the suffering that comes with it.

As new creations in Christ, we have the Holy Spirit and Christ at work within us to overcome temptation and the enticement of sin. However, we will never be able to say we no longer sin because sanctification is not complete until heaven. We should also never give the victory to sin, claiming it has defeated us. Scripture holds these two things in tension as we strive toward Christ-like perfection, even as we are in the midst of being purified through sanctification. This reflects a break with sin where it is no longer our love, but God is.

It is vitally important to know the truth as it relates to sin, since we will never be free of it. The apostle Paul battled no longer being a slave to sin, yet never being able to attain perfection as long as we walk the earth.

*I can already hear your next question: "Does that mean I can't even trust what is good [that is, the law]? Is good just as dangerous as evil?" No again! Sin simply did what sin is so famous for doing: using the good as a cover to tempt me to do what would finally destroy me. By hiding within God's good commandment, sin did far more mischief than it could ever have accomplished on its own. I can anticipate the response that is coming: "I know that all God's commands are spiritual, but I'm not. Isn't this also your experience?" Yes. I'm full of myself—after all, I've spent a long time in sin's prison. What I don't understand about myself is that I decide one way, but then I act another, doing things I absolutely despise. So if I can't be trusted to figure out what is best for myself and then do it, it becomes obvious that God's command is necessary. But I need something **more**! For if I know the law but still can't keep it, and if the power of sin within me keeps sabotaging my best intentions, I obviously need help! I realize that I don't have what it takes. I can will it, but I can't **do** it. I decide to do good, but I don't **really** do it; I decide not to do bad, but then I do it anyway. My decisions, such as they are, don't result in actions. Something has gone wrong deep within me and gets the better of me every time. It happens so regularly* *that it's predictable. The moment I decide to do good, sin is there to trip me up. I truly delight in God's commands, but it's pretty obvious that not all of me joins in that delight. Parts of me covertly rebel, and just when I least expect it, they take charge. I've tried everything and nothing helps.*

I'm at the end of my rope. Is there no one who can do anything for me? Isn't that the real question? The answer, thank God, is that Jesus Christ can and does. He acted to set things right in this life of contradictions where I want to serve God with all my heart and mind, but am pulled by the influence of sin to do something totally different.

Romans 7:13-25, MSG, emphasis added

This is the battle royale that seems to trip us up so often. If we want to be able to stand against the enemy, even when it seems like he could prevail, we have to know the truth. We have to know that sin can cause suffering, but God can use even that. The thing about facing trials with sin is that we also inevitably grow, producing fruits of the Spirit.

Make no mistake: we may tend toward apathy, we may be plagued with depression, fight unhealthy habits, and battle the fleshly desires that resulted as part of the fall, but that junk no longer has the final word.

chapter 5: the truth is...
we must take responsibility

the struggle is real

chapter 5: the truth is…we must take responsibility

It's easy to want to run from our consequences. Generally, consequences aren't what I would consider fun, but they are a training ground for teaching us to think through our actions to make better, more God-honoring choices.

I was one of those kids who showed up in church every time the doors were open, and it wasn't because my parents dragged me. Yes, they encouraged me to be involved in the church, but I was the one who wanted to be there. God captivated my heart at a young age, and I just wanted to be in His presence. As a child, I figured the best way to do that was to be in church every time there was an opportunity.

I was involved in the girls' missions program where we learned about missionaries, how to support them and how to make it a career. I was also involved in the children's choir program, which I loved, because, to me, it meant putting on a show. I was convinced I belonged in spectacular productions (I was not short on self-confidence in those days…or any days, really).

When I was in the fourth grade, my cousins began coming to church with me, which meant they found themselves in the same children's choir. My cousins, one a mere nine months older and the other eighteen months younger than me, were not wired like me. This totally wasn't their scene, so they got the bright idea to skip out on choir. Their proposal was to instead go to the kitchen, find some food, go to the playground and play a bit. If we found snails, we could peel them off the wall and play with them (whatever that meant).

Up to this point, I was the responsible, rule-following one of the three, and I felt like it was my responsibility to take care of them and help guide them on the path of righteousness. In this case, that looked like skipping choir and making sure they didn't get into too much trouble.

Every week for six weeks my parents would drop us off and watch us walk into the building. We would put on a great show, and once we were inside, we would head straight to the church kitchen, rummage around for food, then start our hour of playing. At the end of the hour, we would be sure to walk out the doors as though we were exactly where we were supposed to be when my parents arrived to pick us up. Truth be told, I knew it was wrong, but I kept going with them week after week. When my parents asked how choir rehearsal was, without hesitation, I would respond with, "It was good!" or something to that effect.

It may have remained that way for the better part of the fall, had it not been for my parents sharing a Sunday School class with our choir teacher.

"We've sure missed Keagan in choir. Is everything okay?"

Now, I wasn't there for this conversation, but I can imagine my mom standing there stunned but wise enough to gather information.

"Yes. She's been in choir, though."

"Oh, no. We haven't seen her in about six weeks."

I don't know how the conversation went from there, but what I do know is that Sunday when I got home from church, I changed clothes and went to the car for the fun afternoon my father and I had planned. While I was changing, my mom had a chance to tell my dad about the conversation she'd had that morning. Had she not been wise enough to wait until we got home, I might not have made it home from church.

My dad walked out the door, and I thought we were on our way. He opened the car door, and with his deep voice, I heard, "You need to come inside. We need to talk about choir."

I tried to keep a brave and guiltless face, but inside, I entered flight mode. I began calculating ways out of what I knew was about to be a mess.

When we got inside, my mom was in the living room waiting for us. Dad asked, "So, how has choir been lately?"

"It's been good," I said. I continued on with a completely made-up account of what the last six weeks had looked like in choir to prove I had been there. I wasn't about to get caught in that trap!

"Are you sure? Your teacher told us this morning she hasn't seen you in six weeks."

Dang it. I was caught. But it wasn't my fault! I immediately threw my cousins under the bus, but that didn't exactly save me. For the next who knows how long, my mom and dad explained to me my punishment and why just because I was influenced by my cousins, that didn't make it their fault. Not only had I lied about being in choir, but I had lied again to cover it up when I was caught.

For the next six weeks, I was grounded from breathing, it seemed. I couldn't do anything! I came straight home from school, went to my room, did my homework, and when I was done with that, I had to read. I couldn't watch television, I couldn't go anywhere with friends, I didn't get to go to dance classes, and I had to apologize not only to my choir teacher but to the entire choir…in front of the entire choir.

It was explained to me how not only was this a safety issue, but it was an issue of trust. I no longer had the trust of my parents, and I had to earn it back. I learned later that, had I told the truth the first time I was asked, I would have had a less severe punishment.

The next time I skipped any sort of class was in college when I went home sick because I could barely walk, but other than that, I never skipped again.

Covering a sin with another sin does us no favors. In fact, our hole is only dug deeper when we refuse to bring our sin into the light so it might be exposed to the truth.

Story after story in the Bible recounts this truth. David and Bathsheba. Cain and Abel. Jonah. Adam and Eve. Ananias and Sapphira…

We learn about Ananias and Sapphira in Acts 5. They were husband and wife, and they were among the members of the early church. This couple lived among the believers as first-hand witnesses to Christ-followers taking care of each other, giving of themselves voluntarily. Ananias and Sapphira were among those members of the church who owned land. When members of the early church would sell a piece of property, they would take a gift to the apostles to distribute among those in need.

The two secretly chose to keep part of their earnings for themselves. In a lie, Ananias presented the gift as the entirety of their earnings. When confronted about it, he still chose to cover the lie with yet another lie. He refused to take responsibility for the first lie, and he was struck dead on the spot. Later, his wife Sapphira was confronted about the same thing, and she too chose to lie to cover their sins. The consequence? She was struck dead as well.

Ananias and Sapphira refused to take responsibility for their actions by confessing their mistakes, and they faced the consequences. These consequences were a lesson to others, encouraging them to take responsibility for their actions so their fate might not be the same.

While it is the duty of believers to hold each other accountable, we bear a responsibility for our personal sins, and we are the only ones who can answer for them. The Bible puts it this way, "For each will have to bear his own load" (Galatians 6:5, ESV). To clarify, Adam Clarke in his commentary on Galatians 6 says, "All must answer for themselves, not for their neighbors. And every man must expect to be dealt with by the Divine Judge…Every man must give an account of himself to God." Make no mistake; Christ paid our debt on the cross, and while that grants us freedom from eternal damnation, we are not freed from the consequences of our actions. God is a loving Father who disciplines His children.

He is looking to grow us in maturity, and part of that is taking responsibility for our actions. We can never confess our sins if we are not willing to take responsibility for them.

Much like I did with my cousins in the fourth grade, we often make mistakes that lead us into sin because we listen to the wrong voices. We choose to listen to our flesh or other voices that sound right and seek their will rather than God's.

There are times when it seems like we are taking responsibility by seeking what we claim as the Lord's will. The truth is, our own zeal and impatience can cause impulsive actions which lead to putting what should be our responsibility onto another person. It's like saying our sin is someone else's fault. Our sin is always our responsibility alone, and we are the ones who must be sanctified through it. But, like our sin affects those around us, so does our sanctification.

My first job out of college was a campus missionary internship for our local Baptist student ministry. I loved my job, and I was working incredibly hard to handle situations Biblically. At the start of the second semester, I gained two new co-workers, and I felt like one of them was sort of encroaching on my territory.

Truth be told, I started out mad at this particular co-worker. I felt like there was a level of fake faith, as if the person was putting on a show. I didn't really like that, nor did I like the fact that it seemed like those who interacted with this co-worker were changed, and not for the better.

I carried these things with me for a while, but I made sure I prayed through them because I knew that was the best course of action. However, I didn't exactly listen for the response. I was only concerned with saying I took the right steps.

One day, after our leadership lunch, I took this co-worker into the office, and I blurted out maybe the dumbest thing to ever fall out of my mouth: "I love you, but I do not like you." That brilliant statement was followed by my list of grievances and the justification of how the handling of this situation was Biblical. After all, if you have a problem with someone you should approach them with it, right?

I would be lying if I told you I remember what her response was. I do remember asking if we were good and her saying "yes", but I was not feeling peace. I actually felt in my spirit that things were worse.

A few days later, I got called into the office by our boss to talk about the situation. I sat down in the well-worn chair that had been occupied by what seemed like millions of students and interns before me. I knew something was wrong, but I did not expect what followed.

"I am not happy with you." For whatever reason, this nearly hurt worse than if it were coming from my own father. I respected our boss, and I thought I was growing so much.

He continued on by telling me about how my co-worker had come to him feeling hurt, confused, and unsure how to proceed. He asked me about our conversation, and to be honest, I really wanted to deny everything. However, I knew that if I did, nothing would get better, nor would it be a godly choice to make. I took responsibility for my actions by telling him I had prayed about it, and I thought it was the course of action that was Biblical.

At no point did I seek out wise counsel. I never paused to consider the context of the instruction. Ultimately, I sought to make the Word fit my own agenda. All of this was exposed in the meeting with my boss. He firmly told me I should check the logs in my own eyes, he asked me the hard questions about why I was feeling this way, and he gave me the worst homework in the world: go to my coworker and admit my wrong, genuinely seeking to reconcile.

At that moment, I recognized genuine reconciliation required me to continually take responsibility for my actions. Dang it.

backwards thinking

Here's the deal: as we go about our lives, working out our salvation, learning what it means to take responsibility so we may be sanctified, it becomes incredibly simple to measure our level of suffering against our righteousness—or others' righteousness, for that matter.

It would seem a favorite tactic of the enemy is to make us believe the trials we endure are somehow a direct reflection of our holiness. The father of lies would have us believe the more trials we endure, the holier we are. Or, maybe he would like for us to believe the more trials we endure, the more holy we need to become as if to expose sin.

To some degree, all are true. Because we are believers, we will endure trials, as Jesus did, for the sake of the gospel and becoming more like Him. We also endure trials as a consequence of sin. Let us be sure to remember, however, "it is not true…to say that the personal suffering of any one person is a direct result of that person's sin. The book of Job makes it plain that a person cannot know the moral reasons for another's suffering. God alone knows (Job 42:2, 42:7). If suffering is not a measure of a person's sin, freedom from suffering is not a measure of a person's righteousness."

The reality is the way we think about enduring trials and suffering is often easily distorted. We think with our finite human minds, and we are led to believe our suffering is somehow a direct reflection of our own righteousness, or lack thereof. The enemy counts on that, you know. He keeps relying on the same bag of tricks to cause our spirals in the midst of suffering.

We must quit refusing to root our feelings in truth lest they run rampant. Our feelings take the path of least resistance if we don't boss them around. Therefore, we have to capture them and make them submissive to truth.

We must quit believing the lie that we are less righteous and less loved by God if we mess up. We have the gift of conviction because of the Holy Spirit, but we don't have to dwell on all the ways we botched things and allow guilt to reign in our minds.

We must quit letting the enemy get away with the same tricks and correct our thinking. Where the Accuser twists God's words and manipulates them, we must course correct, playing the Word back to him. It is then that he flees. Where he counts on uninformed and unmanaged emotion, we must rely on truth that never changes, regardless of circumstance. We have to remind that scoundrel that our God is constant. It is only then that we can turn our minds to thinking correctly.

Isaiah 26:3 declares, "You keep him in perfect peace whose mind is stayed on you…" (ESV). Our mind's focus must relentlessly and unapologetically be on the Father or else we are quickly spun around to the path of deception.

Our minds must constantly be steered toward the truth. Our righteousness is not based on our works or anything in us. We have to abandon the idea that our trials reflect our righteousness. Yes, trials expose areas in which we need sanctification. Sometimes, remember, these trials are also due to the fact that we faithfully follow Christ. Enduring trials is hard enough on its own, friend, so quit giving the enemy a foothold with backward thinking!

chapter 6: the truth about trials & growth

the struggle is real

chapter 6: the truth about trials & growth

If you reference a dictionary, you will find the following definition for the word "promise."

> promise (noun)
> prom·ise | \ 'prä-məs \
> 1a: a declaration that one will do or refrain from doing something specified
> b: a legally binding declaration that gives the person to whom it is made a right to expect or to claim the performance or forbearance of a specified act
> 2: reason to expect something: ground for expectation of success, improvement

By that logic, if something is promised, we can bank on it. A promise is as good as a guarantee.

Except when it's not.

Too many times we fall victim to empty promises; from missed little league games to bad habits that never change. The promises come from sinful humans who often write checks they can't cash.

Unlike His creation, God keeps His promises. He is literally the only One we can count on to not let us down because that is not His character. So, when God makes a promise, we can take that to the bank.

Peter tells the Church, "Beloved, do not be surprised at the fiery trial *when* it comes upon you to test you, as though something strange were happening to you" (1 Peter 4:12, ESV, emphasis added). Peter was offering encouragement to fellow believers as they faced trials. It's interesting to note the tone with which Peter addressed this situation. Trials were commonplace for believers, and these served a purpose.

The truth is, because we are Christians, we are promised suffering. It may come in the form of a broken promise, a cancer diagnosis, or maybe a string of things just not going the way we plan. Nevertheless, it will come.

While that sounds discouraging, and you may be thinking, "Wow. What a promise…", take heart! Reminding us why we are promised trials to endure, the Bible says, "for you know that the testing of your faith produces steadfastness. And let steadfastness have its full effect, that you may be perfect and complete, lacking in nothing" (James 1:3-4, ESV). While we are in the midst of the muck and mire, God is at work producing good things in us. God is accomplishing the main goal of sanctification: that we would be made more like Christ. If we are to be made like Christ, we have to think and behave like He did. But how?

Do me a favor. Think of your hero growing up.

Chances are you—like me—watched every move that person made. You wanted to imitate that person in every way you could. You watched the way your hero walked, heard the way he or she spoke, practiced the hobbies you saw that idol do, and you wanted so badly to be just like him or her. You studied your hero, to the most minute detail, picking up some of the habits and mannerisms you observed. The more time you spent with them, the more you became like them.

That's what we are called to as Christians. We are beckoned to spend time with the Lord, observe His movements, study His interactions, and follow His examples. This is literally the name we were given when we became His: Christian, meaning little Christ.

At every turn, we are given an opportunity to wear this name tag well and to showcase whose we are. It may be by offering grace to those who have wronged us, especially when we would rather hold a grudge, or it may be the way we weather the storms.

You see, trials serve as a sort of proving ground for our faith. In 1 Peter 1:7 we see "that the tested genuineness of [our] faith—more precious than gold that perishes though it is tested by fire—may be found to result in praise and glory and honor at the revelation of Jesus Christ" (ESV). The Greek word used for "tested genuineness" is *dokimazo*, which means to "test, examine, prove, scrutinize to see whether a thing is genuine or not." As we are tested, we begin to bear more abundant, healthy fruit. This tells us everything we need to know about why God allows trials to enter our lives: it is how our faith grows in steadfastness that it may glorify God.

Unfortunately, these trials do not simply flip a switch in us. It takes time. Sanctification, whether through facing the consequences of our sin or through testing that we may grow, is a process that constantly transforms us. I am not the same person I was ten years ago, two years ago, two months ago, or even two weeks ago. It isn't about who we were but who we are becoming because God loves us enough to meet us where we are. He also loves us enough to challenge us. We work out our faith and grow in our faith, broadening our understanding of God. This sanctification is one thing we can count on this side of heaven; it never ends.

While that may sound discouraging, it proves the main point of our lives. Our lives are not about us. Instead, they are about God. Our suffering bears witness to God's capability. Even as weak and broken humans, we get the privilege of showcasing Him.

In general, we are familiar with 2 Corinthians 12:9-10: "But he said to me, 'My grace is sufficient for you, for my power is made perfect in weakness.' Therefore, I will boast all the more gladly of my weaknesses, so that the power of Christ may rest upon me" (ESV).

Let's not lose the beauty of this scripture with its overuse! The grace of God is always present in our lives, regardless of the difficulty of our circumstances. He does not leave us to our own devices, nor does He leave us to drown under the pressure we might be facing. Instead, He shows up in ways we cannot imagine to be enough, to provide and to carry us. We don't have to be enough on our own because He is at work in us, telling His story through our everyday lives.

When we don't sleep much the night before a big day and feel like we will not be able to make it, He is there.

When we lose our cool with the kids because they won't listen, He is there.

the truth about trials & growth

When we receive the cancer diagnosis, He is there.

When we face the consequences of our sin, He is there.

When we have to sit in our brokenness, He is there.

When we have to make the difficult decision to quit our jobs, He is there.

When we struggle with our purpose, He is there.

When we battle mental or chronic illness, disability, He is there.

When it doesn't *feel* like He is there, the *truth* is, He is.

Big suffering or small, our God provides us enough grace to walk through the trials of our lives. All the while, He is at work because He sees the bigger picture.

the struggle is real

chapter 7: in order to grow - pruning & crushing

the struggle is real

chapter 7: in order to grow - pruning & crushing

Each year, I look forward to spring when I get to pick out plants. Over the years, I have learned what I am good at growing and what I am good at killing. I search the garden centers every year looking for a few new, fun plants I might like to try my hand at, but I always give a hot pink gerbera daisy, a dew plant, and petunias a home in my gardening pots. I look forward to the colors and growth throughout the season, and I love when I pull into the driveway and see the plants greeting me with what seems like a big smile. It's a sign of life at our house. Sometimes, these few little plants even provide me with a sense of serenity as I water them and prune them after a long day.

Every gardener or vinedresser knows that in order to produce the best, most abundant fruit, the plant must be pruned. While I have never been a vinedresser, I know this to be true with my petunias. Each season, I see my petunias burst forth with their beautiful colors, bloom a few days, and as other blooms are opening, I see blooms shutting and shriveling. When I see those blooms close in on themselves, I know it is time to remove those once vibrant flowers.

While it's a simple and seemingly insignificant task, plucking the bloom from its stem, it is necessary to perpetuate growth.

If the dead blooms are not removed, the plant wastes energy that could be used to grow the beautiful new blooms trying to create life in the now-dead bloom. When this happens, the growth of the plant is stifled.

In John 15:1-7, Jesus makes it clear we are much the same way. If we are to grow in Him, we must be pruned. Our energy must go toward producing good, healthy fruit rather than wasting our energy on things that either do not benefit us or ultimately harm us because what we feed grows. It is the goal that anything that does not point to Jesus, that hinders us from showing Him and growing in Him, is cut away so we may thrive.

Make no mistake. This is not always an easy or pleasant process. In fact, we will often resist this process because we are creatures who gravitate toward comfort. However, if we are to live our lives in a way that allows us to continually grow in Christ, we must find our uncomfort zone.

If you're anything like me, you aren't about to go hunt down a situation that makes you uncomfortable. Instead, you are going to stay in a safe bubble, potentially sticking one toe out every now and then to smile at a stranger. The truth is, though, we are called to more. That's part of why God allows us to experience trials.

God knows that trials put us to the test, stressing us in ways that expose the parts of us that are no longer producing good fruit; those parts that must be removed so we can continue to grow. When these things that thrive in the dark where they hide are finally exposed, we have no choice but to deal with them so they may no longer hinder us as we work towards growth.

It seems, though, as I prune my petunias to aid their growth, they tend to thrive. It's not uncommon for petunias to outgrow their environment in the course of the growing season. You see, good and beautiful things require pruning, too. So, when this outgrowing occurs, I have two choices: I can either transfer the plant to a new, larger pot, or I can cut the plant back, allowing it to grow again in that same planter.

Should I replant the petunias in a larger pot, I give them the opportunity to take more ground. But they can't do that without letting their roots graft into the new soil. They must struggle to establish their new home. On the other hand, if I cut the plant back but allow it to remain in the same planter, I limit the ground the petunias are able to take but still allow growth.

In the same way, God does good and beautiful work in us that grows us. Sometimes, as we abide in Him to produce good fruit, He allows us to take more ground. Other times, as we abide in Him, we continue to grow, but the ground we take may be limited. Our job is simply to faithfully abide in Christ as He does the pruning so we may look most like Him.

crushing

"I need you out of the house by May 15. We will be doing renovations." The screen of my phone lit up with a text message from our landlord, as we crawled into bed for the night.

My mind began to reel. We had been living in this house for a year and a half and never missed a payment. We paid for all the repairs made to the house. We never gave any indication of wanting to leave. We took care of the place. What did we do? Why, all of the sudden, did we need renovations? Where would we go?

I was stunned, borderline mad.

"Ummm…okay?" was all the message I could muster.

My husband could tell something was not quite right, so he sat up in bed and asked, "Is everything okay?"

The floodgates opened. Not only did I tell him about the message I'd just received from our landlord, but I spilled out all the thoughts that were racing through my mind. "She wants us out of here in less than two weeks, and we don't even know what our next plan is. I know we're looking for jobs, but we don't know if we will be here or in another city. We can't very well rent a place for two or three months; places lease for six months at least. We can't afford much right now, so where will we even be able to go?! How in the world will we get packed in that amount of time? It's not like we did anything wrong. We've always been on time with our payments. We've fixed everything, been easy to work with, and have taken care of the place. We've done everything we could to be good renters. Why would she not wait until we move out? Why, all of the sudden, do they need to do renovations?" Each thought rolled over the previous one, never giving any time to process.

Understand this: my husband doesn't get worked up about much. As I stumbled over the pile of thoughts trying to make their way out, he just listened. Finally, when I was done, he said, "It's okay. We will figure it out. Yes, it's a lot to process. There are so many things to figure out in not a lot of time, but we have to trust that God knows what is coming." I took that as comfort, and I crawled into bed. I was emotionally exhausted and still upset. I felt betrayed and somewhat guilty since we were being evicted.

The next day, we told my parents about the situation. We threw around our ideas, our initial thoughts, and came up with very little. Our last resort option seemed to be the only option: move in with my parents until we could find another option, at least for the foreseeable future.

In the midst of packing up all of our things to store, I had a job interview to teach at a middle school in our town. When I was offered the job, I did not feel at peace about it, so I turned it down. I couldn't help but think, *Oh, great. That was a sure thing. We could've finally had a plan.* At the same time, my husband had interview after interview with no job offers.

The tension continued to mount. We were getting down to the wire. If we didn't get hired soon, we wouldn't be—at least not for this school year.

Finally, my husband received a call from his hometown principal asking both of us to come for an interview. While I agreed to go, I was not excited, to say the least. I did not think this was where either of us needed to be, but I knew if we didn't go, we could never say we tried everything.

On the spot, we were both offered jobs. While I felt better about the situation after the interview, I didn't really want to move to this town to live. I couldn't shake the feeling this new town in which I was so adamantly opposed to living was where we were supposed to be. It was the same nudge that told me not to take the initial job offer. We had to move, and at least now we had a direction. We could start looking for places to rent.

As we began to search for homes, we realized this was just

another struggle in this string of adversities. Not only was there limited availability for rental houses, but they were also all far beyond what we felt we could afford. When we finally found one we thought we might be able to afford, it had been rented just twenty minutes prior. There was nowhere else.

I broke.

I found myself on my parents' front porch, in the heat of the day, throwing a fit. I was audibly praying through each sob.

"God." I didn't know what I had to say from there. I was mad. I was sad. I was desperate. I was tired. I didn't want to say anything I might regret.

"God." I paused to breathe through my flood of tears. "God, I don't understand. Why?"

I paused, trying to gather my thoughts, trying to make them coherent. With tears still streaming down my face in the sweltering heat, I proceeded. "Why are we here? First, we did everything right, but we still got evicted from our house. We had nowhere to go. If it weren't for my parents, we might be living on the street or in the storage building with our stuff. Then, I got a job offer, and YOU made me say no. Then, we went to the last place on earth either of us wanted to be, and YOU told us, 'This is it, kids.' Are you kidding me? Now, we're trying to be obedient, but we still don't have a place to live. We can't afford any of our options, and they are all in not great parts of town. Why? Why can we not catch a break? Why does it feel like every time we turn around something else goes wrong?"

I needed to breathe, to stop, and listen. What else could I do?

As I sat, I realized all of this came down to one thing. I felt overwhelmed, crushed, and out of control. Not one of these things was within my limited control. It dawned on me, at that moment, I needed to be in a place where I felt safe. I needed refuge to run to where I knew I could fall apart. I needed a place where I knew I could surrender control. I needed to know all the things that felt overwhelming would not end up overtaking me.

As I listened, I heard a still small voice whisper in my spirit, "Child, it's me. Trust me, your Refuge and Strength." While this was the truth I knew already, it was as though I had an epiphany.

In these moments, I realized, we cannot be our own shelter. On our own, we are not enough. We are humans who are limited in perspective and power, without an ability to supernaturally orchestrate any number of things to work together just so. But God can. As we go through trials, it can be overwhelming and feel crushing, but God is our Refuge and Strength.

When we are overwhelmed, being crushed by the weight of this life, we can run to God with the truth of Psalm 91:4 as our map.

He will cover you with his pinions, and under his wings you will find refuge; his faithfulness is a shield and buckler.
Psalm 91:4, ESV

This verse is rich with the protections God provides us through the trials we face, regardless of how trivial they may seem. Here, we are literally told the Almighty will take us under His wing to protect us, his children. There, we are promised safety. But our Father doesn't stop there. He remains; He is faithful. That alone gives a sense of protection. We are surrounded by His protection. Minister and author Matthew Henry echoes this idea when he wrote, "Great security is promised to every believer in the midst of danger...Whatever is done, our heavenly Father's will is done; and we have no reason to fear...though trouble and afflictions befall, it shall come, not for his hurt, but for good."

In the midst of our trials, we are not promised fairy tales and rainbows. Instead, we are promised protection. We are promised safety. Still, we must be cautious in our understanding of this promise.

First, we must realize our earthly view of protection is not the same as the protection that comes with a relationship with Christ. In our flesh, we hear the promise of protection and breathe a sigh of relief, thinking we get out of all our trials unscathed. Unfortunately, that's not true. While God holds us close, sheltering us, He is still at work sanctifying us. If He never allowed us to walk through the hard things, we would never be changed, and we would certainly never realize our need for a Savior. Instead, our understanding of the protection of our King ultimately comes to the realization that, in the end, we win because "the God of peace will shortly bruise Satan under our feet" (Romans 16:20, ESV). When we think with the mind of Christ, we remember our adoption as sons and daughters of God allows us to live protected by the hope of heaven. Because of that, our lives are protected with the hope of heaven.

We also must understand the social cliché, "God won't give you more than you can handle," is a lie straight from the pit of hell. If God never gave us more than we could handle, we would have no need for a Savior, nor would there be anyone struggling. Life would be a breeze. Friend, don't let scripture taken out of context be your life raft. When that happens, it is no longer truth. It no longer has the power of God.

> *No temptation has overtaken you that is not common to man. God is faithful, and he will not let you be tempted beyond your ability, but with the temptation, he will also provide a way of escape, that you may be able to endure it.*
> 1 Corinthians 10:13, ESV

Go back and read that again, paying close attention to the words.

While this is the verse that is often used to tell us that God doesn't give us more than we can handle, we skim over the fact that this isn't about trials. Instead, Paul is teaching about the idea of temptation. Taking Scripture out of context puts us—and others in our wake—in a dangerous position. In fact, in our discouragement, we can feel like we aren't measuring up, or we may even ignore our suffering, thinking we can handle it on our own.

When it comes to temptation, we have a choice: we can either allow ourselves to fall to temptation, or we can run from it through the escape route God provides. This is not the case with suffering. We often don't have a choice, unless of course our suffering is a consequence of our own dumb choices.

While we are likely to feel like we can't handle temptation, our God is near, providing the way out. The same is true for each trial we face. It's understandable to cry out to God, feeling like we are drowning. In fact, that is where we find our ever faithful God, no matter how far away He seems.

The apostle Paul understood these things well. In his early ministry, he fled several towns, as people looked to persecute him. He was arrested countless times for sharing the gospel. He was thrown in jail and left for dead, and yet he found shelter under the wings of God. This shelter did not excuse him from being beaten and experiencing other suffering, nor did it excuse him from dying the death of a martyr. Instead, knowing he did not suffer alone, provided him encouragement. Each time he was tossed in jail, he waited to see his fate with peace in his soul because he knew God had his back.

In our Refuge, we find peace, regardless of the storms that rage around us. Isaiah 26:3 says, "You keep him in perfect peace whose mind is stayed on you because he trusts in you" (ESV). Our Refuge is never far away; all that is required of us is to keep our eyes on Him. He will guide our steps and show us that because He is God, and we are His, all that seems to be crushing us will not overtake us.

But even if you should suffer for righteousness' sake, you will be blessed. Have no fear of them, nor be troubled, but in your hearts honor Christ the Lord as holy, always being prepared to make a defense to anyone who asks you for a reason for the hope that is in you...
1 Peter 3:14-17, ESV

When we are faced with hard questions like why God allows bad things to happen to good people, we may encounter hesitation and skepticism when we start spouting off Scriptures. However, if we can share our experience of who God is and how He walked through trials with us, we are able to show off our God. People need to know that God is for them. He is not actively working against us.

When God moved us out of our little rental house, He was preparing us for our next steps. Being kicked out allowed us to be more mobile as we followed His call, and while we waited in desperation, we saw Him answer prayers. He provided a place to live, in a good neighborhood, at two-thirds less than we were expecting to pay each month in rent. The place had three bedrooms to allow for visitors, and it perched itself at the edge of a field for our dog to run in and us to see the beautiful sunrises. He carried us through what seemed like persecution by providing a place of solace.

Ever heard of the persecuted Church? (Hint: it isn't the Church in America.)

All across the world, there are Christians who live in fear for their lives, knowing the consequence of being a Christian is death. They live in genuine fear for their lives. These are those who have risked it all to follow Jesus. While that may sound dramatic, similar events occurred throughout Scripture. It should come as no surprise, then, that we are told over and over throughout the Scriptures that we will face persecution for His name, up to and including our very lives. It is no secret that this persecution is to be expected. But the experience of persecution is not to be confused with the notion that God is working against us.

While trials can be a result of sin or proving of our faith, the purpose is the same: that we become more like Christ each day. As we become more like Christ, we are able to see the world as He does, beginning to embrace trials for the work they accomplish in us.

the struggle is real

chapter 8: in order to grow - practicing humility & perseverance

the struggle is real

chapter 8: in order to grow - practicing humility & perseverance

When I was a kid, I always associated the word "humility" with humiliation. I was certain they were somehow related. It wasn't until a few years ago that I had the revelation that humility doesn't equal humiliation. However, in that same moment, I understood why I associated the two so closely.

It is likely we've all heard the phrase, "Pride comes before a fall." Sometimes, it is used as a warning from those who have gone before us, as they recognize pride and arrogance in us. Other times, we hear it in passing, as a reminder to keep ourselves in check to avoid arrogance. It's one of those quick-witted quips that, while true, has become cliché and overused. To our dismay, it is one of those sayings that hurts when we actually come face to face with learning the depth of truth found in the words.

Being hard-headed, I have been forced to reconcile with this truth on many occasions, but most often, it has not been a quick lesson.

It takes a special person to balance that out in me, and thankfully, my husband has that ability. Over the course of our marriage, he has worked diligently to lovingly expose the pride in me, pointing out the arrogance of my tone or my words. And trust me—he knows what that's like because one of the things we have always worked hard to make a priority in our marriage is constant and direct communication.

Of course, his goal is never to embarrass me when he points out my lack of humility; I do that on my own.

The most vivid memory I have of this is the night of our rehearsal dinner.

We were preparing to start the rehearsal, and the entire wedding party had been told what seemed like forty-seven times where they needed to be. My husband, our wedding coordinator, and I had to stop by the sound booth to go over a few final details before we started. I expected everyone to be ready to go as soon as we turned around. I'd already asked multiple times, the entire place knew we were limited on time, and they certainly knew my method of operation: organized and scheduled.

After what was no more than a two-minute conversation, I flipped around in my 1950's tulle gown, ready to run through the plan for the next day. I couldn't seem to find any of the groomsmen and a family member who needed to know their role for the next day. In my irritation, I made a quick, snide comment, just loud enough for my future husband and wedding coordinator to hear.

Up until this point, I had worked hard to not be a Bridezilla, but she escaped. I knew it as soon as I opened my mouth. Of course, I didn't want to make a scene, so I just kept moving while pretending to ignore it. Maybe nobody else noticed. Except, I wasn't that lucky because God knew I needed accountability.

"Keagan." I sheepishly glanced toward the man who had bravely agreed to be my husband the next day.

"What?" I wish I could say this was a calm, knowing question, and the conversation would be terminated here, but it wasn't. Instead, I snapped back a bit to cover my embarrassment about the fact I had even an ounce of Bridezilla in me.

"Attitude. Down a notch." There was a look of fire in his eyes that was subtle but told me he meant business. Yet, there was no part of me that wanted to defend myself or to argue back. I fell in line, giving a look of apology to my husband.

While the conversation lasted no more than thirty seconds, it was burned in my brain. Who in the world could talk to me like that and have me submit? The better question, though: how did I know this was conviction, a pride check, if you will?

Only Jesus.

Looking back, this is the moment that is seared into my memory as God beginning to refine my mouth outrunning my brain since that's the thing that seems to be one of my biggest sources of humiliation. I speak before I think too often.

Over the years, I am reminded of times I should have kept my mouth shut. I feel instant guilt. I've sat next to my husband at football games as he has nudged me to keep my mouth shut so as not to humiliate myself, and while it has sometimes been helpful, there have been times I've paid attention to those nudges too late, only to be humiliated in a later conversation.

I've worked hard over the last eight years of our marriage to remember these instances. I've wanted so desperately to quit feeling guilty over the things I shouldn't have said. I'm quicker to pay attention to not just the nudges of my husband, but those of the Holy Spirit.

I desire to honor my husband and the Lord with the words that come out of my mouth, and it has been a lesson I have had to learn—I need to be more cautious to keep my words in check before they escape my mouth.

Still, eight years later, I remain in progress, as I hear the stinging words, "I guess I just need to be more careful about what I share with you." Hot tears burn my face. I thought I had been doing so well to keep my mouth shut, yet I overshared because I was too quick to share a story with more details than I was at liberty to disclose.

"I've been working so hard. I thought I was doing so well. I'm so sorry." Again, I found myself embarrassed and humiliated. I treasured this relationship with my husband and wanted to honor it, yet here I was again. Still in progress. At that moment, I thought of the people I admire who know just what to say and how to say it without an ounce of pride; they literally serve the world around them from a place of humility. Why couldn't I be that way, exhibiting humility as a positive character trait rather than jumping straight to humiliation?

In fact, I want to exhibit the type of humility that is encouraged by the writers of the New Testament, as it is exemplified throughout the life of Jesus Christ Himself. As I read through the account in Matthew 26-27, I am struck by the humility it took for Him to go to the cross. Here, we see the humility of Christ as He prays in the garden. Three times, Jesus tells the Father He doesn't want to go to the cross, yet, He yields Himself obediently to whatever God says. Then, as He is arrested, He does not resist. Instead, He willingly goes with those who came to take Him to the cross. He doesn't stop there, though. He continues to remain silent when He is accused instead of defending Himself. He allows Himself to be beaten, mocked, spit on, and hanged on a cross without defense, offering Himself for not only death but being forsaken by His own Father. All of this He did for us, setting aside His desire to avoid the indescribable pain and ultimate wrath of God. He set the example of humility by not only washing feet (John 13:5) but dying in our place so we may have life.

God is at work to make us the best versions of ourselves, the ones that look most like Him. Because He is not proud, it is His desire that we are not proud. He allows trials to prune away the branches that produce pride. He wants our vines to produce humbleness. Unfortunately, we are too often blinded to our pruning because living a life of humility looks, well… humiliating. It looks like serving others ahead of ourselves: washing their dirt-stained feet, getting out in the cold to serve a hot meal, opening up our homes to strangers. It's actually seeing the "least of these" (Matthew 25:40) as well as those who are masquerading behind a beautiful costume that says, "I'm fine."

The Bible puts it best in James 4:6 saying, "Therefore it says, 'God opposes the proud, but gives grace to the humble'" (ESV). God is so serious about creating in us a spirit of humility that He will allow trials in our lives that do, for lack of a better word, humiliate us. In this way, the fruit of humility begins to take residence in our lives.

the struggle is real

Just ask the apostle Paul. In 2 Corinthians 12:7, Paul tells the church at Corinth God gave him a constant reminder of just how human and just how vulnerable he was so he would not boast in himself. With the focus off of himself, Paul was able to glorify God all the more.

When we face trials, it is sometimes due to our own mistakes and our own pride, but God still uses the trials to give us moments of introspection. You see, when we are humiliated, we want to play the blame game. Of course, it is everyone else's fault; we did nothing wrong. When we become tired of fighting, we realize we have to stare down ourselves, often making us reconcile with our pride. When this happens, God doesn't say, "I told you so." He instead offers us a chance to do better. He calls us to lay aside our pride so we may look like Him and spare ourselves humiliation later. Win-win.

perseverance

At any point in time, if I asked myself or any random stranger on the street how they were feeling, it might easily be brushed off. If we're honest and willing to do the work of actually connecting and talking with each other, we might find we are all living in a state of exhaustion.

We are tired of all the politics. We are tired of all the societal pressures we face daily. Even if we don't cave to them, it's still a struggle to fight them. We are tired of everyone's opinions being drenched in hate. We are tired of nobody really listening. We are tired of not being connected to others, even if we are introverts. We are tired of constantly being on the go, even though we can't seem to find anything to remove from our schedules. Our schedules are overwhelmed with busyness and our souls starve.

I learned, when I was a brand new mother, that being tired makes us more susceptible to making poor choices. I began to worry about just surviving and keeping this new, little, crying babe alive. I didn't seem to have time for anything else as I lived my life in three-hour stretches. I couldn't see past three hours, and to be honest, sometimes, I just wanted things to be normal again. It was easier that way. I used to have the time to do the things I wanted to do—to feed my soul and to connect with others. How long would this last? When would we be "normal" again? I asked myself these questions over and over in the first few weeks of motherhood.

In an effort to establish normal, I determined I needed to have rest so I would be able to think clearly, make good decisions, and begin to thrive. The first thing to go? Waking up early to spend time in the Word. Bad plan. This wasn't the intentional move I planned to make, but I let the cries of my sweet girl wake me up for the day instead of an alarm clock to spend time alone with God. From that point on, there was no stopping. I noticed my defenses against the enemy began to wane. I was much more susceptible to believing the lies he so readily fed me. I had no stamina to fight. I had no place I truly found rest. Nothing I was believing was rooted in truth, and I could feel my soul starving.

I knew this couldn't be all there was to this motherhood gig. I desperately wanted sustenance, a place of rest... hope, to know it got better, or easier, anyway. As my girl cuddled on my chest while I rocked her to sleep, I realized the truth that this type of suffering—this ordinary, everyday suffering—often gets overlooked. It's part of who we are, and we so often just keep pushing through until we make it to the other side.

When we feel like we can't catch a break, that things won't ever be normal or somewhat easy again, it's hard to see past the moment. It's hard to remember that in these moments, work is still being done in us to grow our perseverance so we may live our lives well until our work here is done. Even in those moments—those joyously hard, sacred moments—when we look trial in the face, we can see God is building us.

It's no secret the life we live is a hard one, but we can take comfort in the fact that our Savior went through the same things we go through. While our world is different now than when He walked the streets, He is no less privy to our experiences. In fact, in Hebrews 4:15 we are told, "We do not have a high priest who is unable to sympathize with our weaknesses…" (ESV). It is because of this, we can have confidence in the fact we are able to run our races well. Not perfectly but well. In James 1:12, we are encouraged to remain steadfast when trials grace our doorstep. If we do, we are able to reap the rewards of running our race well (Hebrews 10:35-36).

Make no mistake, it's tempting to want to take the easy way out. When we choose that, though, we are cheating ourselves out of letting trials accomplish their work. We miss out on becoming mature in Christ (James 1:3-4).

Romans 5:3-4 says, "Not only that, but we rejoice in our sufferings, knowing that suffering produces endurance, and endurance produces character, and character produces hope" (ESV). Admittedly, when my new little squish cried, this was the last place my mind went. I only had so many tricks up my sleeve to make it stop, and I was too tired to find new ones. Thankfully, given the relief of friends, grandparents, or her new daddy, I could take a step back, take a nap, and think clearly for a moment.

How was I to let God have His full effect in this trial that was new motherhood? How would I let myself press in so I might see that suffering produces endurance, which builds character that sees hope? My first priority had to be realizing this girl I held in my arms was a good gift and remembering she was an answer to so many prayers. Because of that, I was able to recognize that God does not give good gifts or answer prayers in order to make us happy; it's that He may receive glory. Our happiness is a by-product. But happiness or answered prayers do not necessarily equal ease.

I had to reorient my desire for easy and normal and rested to His perspective. It began in the cuddles, coos, and smiles. I saw what my daughter could be—who she could grow up to be if I stewarded my gift well. My thoughts began to shift from "Make it stop!" to, "It has to be hard to learn to be a human. This precious girl is new to this world. How can I help?" This question was met with a whisper, "Come meet with me."

As I prioritized spending time in the Word and looking for God in the ordinary, messy moments, I learned to endure. With each need I met of my daughter's, I saw God meet a need in me, developing my maturity and character. I found joy in chasing Jesus, regardless of how messy it was or what time of day it was. My perspective shifted because I found a real source of rest in Him. Regardless of how sleepy I was, I could now keep my eternal inheritance at the front of my mind so I could press on.

Don't be deceived: There is no "quick fix." It's hard work to build a discipline of pressing in, but as we do, and we let God do the work, He meets us there.

the struggle is real

chapter 9: when trials have their full effect

the struggle is real

chapter 9: when trials have their full effect

Every day, thousands of women see a pregnancy test reveal the information that they will be adding to their family. From the outside looking in, it seems so easy. Or at least, it did.

When we made the decision to pursue expanding our family, I thought it was going to be easy. I figured, at most, we would be pregnant in three months. By the time I got the third negative pregnancy test, I was discouraged. I began wrestling with all the thoughts common to those who struggle to get pregnant. Is something wrong with me? Is something wrong with my husband? Should we be worried about this? Are we doing the right things? How can we mess this up? Why is this taking so long? Am I not worthy enough or good enough to be a mom? I've done all the right things, made all the right choices. Why does it seem like she sneezes and is pregnant? She doesn't even seem to like her kids.

This was the cycle for the next nine months. Try. Wait. Test. Cry. Try. Wait. Test. Cry. Try. Wait. Test. Cry. When I was finally able to see my doctor, we decided to pursue some treatment options to help my body get ready for pregnancy. Apparently, I needed a little bit of assistance, but I was assured this was a relatively normal issue. While I knew that should have been comforting information, I didn't feel comforted.

the struggle is real

Instead, it felt like my body wasn't working. Something was wrong with me. Regardless, it was worth a shot. We would check back in with the doctor in three months.

While there was some predictability now, the one thing I could be certain of during this treatment, it seemed, was the fact the cycle remained the same. Try. Wait. Test. Cry. Try. Wait. Test. Cry. Try. Wait. Test. Cry. Was this treatment not working? Was there a bigger issue? What if I truly couldn't have children?

I found myself in the doctor's office yet again. While I love my doctor, I was hoping to visit with more positive news. I wanted desperately to be discussing our pregnancy journey rather than coming up with a plan to aid in our getting pregnant. Truth be told, I feared something was "wrong" with one of us. Not that we would be the first to have struggles conceiving, but that wasn't part of the narrative I was writing for myself.

My doctor was optimistic. "I'm not quite ready to give up. Let's give it another three months on this treatment, and we can go ahead and set up appointments to explore things further in the meantime." We left with the first of two appointments scheduled. One for me, and one for my husband. We needed to be sure there were no barriers, and if there were, we needed to know what we were up against.

We returned home, discouraged, but at least we had what seemed like more of a plan this time. We kept trying, even though we were significantly busier than when this all started. Having a baby was our priority. It seemed every time we turned around another one of our friends was telling the world their family was expanding, and while I was happy for them, I was also sad for me. Try. Wait. Test. Cry.

"God. I don't know what you're working on, but I'm not really a fan. Why are you not allowing us to get pregnant? What happens if we can't have children of our own?"

Try. Wait. Test. Cry.

"God. I will do whatever you want me to. Is our story one of adoption only?" This was the prayer my heart whispered day after day. I was afraid to talk to my husband about it, mostly because I didn't want it to be true. I wanted to give birth, and I was surprised at how desperate I was to actually birth a child. When I was growing up, I wanted to be a mother, sure, but it wasn't all I wanted to be. Now that I couldn't get pregnant, it seemed that was the only thing I wanted.

Try.

It helped that our schedule was busier. I didn't spend so much time trying to figure out what I could do to get pregnant. After all, we were doing all the right things. We had been for the last seventeen months. This was the month we had our doctor's appointment to check-in before diving a bit deeper into the troubleshooting process.

Wait.

The air was crisp that September afternoon. It had the perfect hint of coolness in it to signal the glory of football season. I found myself walking into the doctor's office in pajamas. It was spirit week, and we prepared for our homecoming game. That night, I planned to find myself in front of our team bonfire after squeezing in this doctor appointment. I sat, waiting, swinging my legs, not really expecting much to happen.

"Well, you should be pregnant by now." My doctor was trying to lighten the mood but in no way meant to be insensitive. "From here, we may want to pursue further testing. I can recommend you to some specialists, so we can get to the bottom of this."

We asked all the questions we could think of, made a plan to follow up our appointments with specialist visits, and before we left, we touched base about where we were in the cycle this month. I knew it was getting close to finding yet another negative on the test, but the doctor encouraged me to take a test at home. He told me he didn't want to test me too early and get a false negative. I agreed and flew out the door to finish the week of excitement before we could finally rest. I knew I wouldn't be taking a test for at least two more days. I just wanted to survive the week and get some sleep so I had enough energy to process the inevitable.

We woke up late that Saturday morning, and I wasn't totally sure I had completely recovered from the hectic week behind us. I was still tired. Groggy and disheveled, I made my way to test.

Test.

I walked back to the bed to rest a bit more. I had to wait for the results anyway, and there was nothing pressing that needed my attention. I forgot about the test and watched tv for a while, ate breakfast, and started to get ready. Oh! There's the test.

when trials have their full effect

I called my husband in for moral support before I actually took a look.

Weep.

This time, my tears were tears of joy and disbelief. We were pregnant! Eighteen months later, and we were finally pregnant!

I spent the morning praising God for the good gift of life growing inside me. I quickly thought about the fear of miscarriage. I couldn't stop smiling, but in the afternoon, I paused to remember all the questions, all the difficulties, all the worry, all the unknowns, and all the times I doubted God. To be honest, I was ashamed of my doubt.

In all the waiting, had we learned nothing? Was our waiting wasted? Did we endure this feeling of God being absent for no reason? Looking back, I wish I could say I hadn't wasted that time, but I spent more time worrying than praying. I desperately wish I'd followed the example of the church in Acts 1. They didn't waste their time or try to move forward too hastily. No. They prayed. They worshiped as they were waiting on God to move.

The lessons we learn in the midst of trials, regardless of how small they may seem, are hard-won. They require us to walk through the fire, all the while calling us to chase hard after Jesus. They give us opportunities to choose obedience. When we choose obedience, we get to walk in freedom, but we must also know that obedience is costly.

When we "learn obedience through what [we] suffer" we come out on the other side with deep-seated convictions

(Hebrews 5:8, ESV). We earn our experience and expertise in the trenches of war. Because of this, it is likely we won't back down from these convictions easily, and these convictions are what guide us in obedience. We act on what we believe.

It may be true that what we believe—what we know to be true through God showing more of Himself to us throughout the struggle—is not popular. We will face opposition, even from those we love. These trials—these moments we choose to persevere and obey rather than giving up—will cost us relationships, opportunities, and dreams we once held so tightly.

It is in these moments, we realize our humanity. We realize how little we are in control and even how vulnerable we are. Hopefully, we realize, on our own, we are not enough. Only God can be enough, and only God can be the one in control. Thankfully, God does not just leave us to waste away in our humanity. Instead, He uses our humanity as a showcase for Him and His glory, because as John 15:5 says, "apart from [Him] we can do nothing" (ESV). When we found ourselves trying to get pregnant, we did all the right things, according to Science. We did all the things we could control. Ultimately, we learned we were not the ones in control; He was.

We found ourselves needing support. We needed people to walk alongside us to let us know we were not the first or the last to experience this. And while it didn't really seem okay, God was at work on our behalf. We learned we cannot go this road alone, even though we tried. While that support was helpful, it wasn't foolproof. Those who choose to champion us will not mean to let us down, but they—like us—were not meant to bear the burden of Christ. We cannot expect our champions to be perfect or to never fail us. We must depend first on the Lord in the midst of any trial. He sends us the resources we need to make it through if we will just depend on Him. Yes, I kept pressing into God, turning to prayer, reading the Word, looking for answers, but I didn't understand the point of this journey.

When trials have their full effect, we are changed. Work has taken place in us that has grown us, sanctified us, and made us look more like Christ. Each time we are stretched, we know God more. While God does this for our good, the work being done in us isn't always only about us. The fact that we didn't have to pursue further testing beyond scheduling appointments sometimes makes me feel a bit ashamed to call our journey a trial. We walked through eighteen months of tears and pain, and while we were never actually told we were infertile, we felt it deeply. Our suffering in those months was used to sanctify us, but it also allowed us to become a resource for others who were struggling with the same thing.

I taught down the hall from a trendy, brunette coach, struggling with severe endometriosis. The summer before we got pregnant, she had surgery to help alleviate some of the challenges this diagnosis was posing so that she, too, could grow a baby. She spent the rest of the next two school years visiting specialist after specialist, holistic doctors, and pursuing treatment options. When I was able to catch her in the hall one spring afternoon, she told me her fears, her options, and where she was in the process. While she tried to stay strong, I recognized the desperation. I recognized the need for encouragement. At that moment, I realized one of the reasons for God allowing this trial to be part of our story. Not only was it meant for our good, but it was meant for the good of this friend.

The point of my battle? It was not that either of us were sinners being punished for something. No, it was because of the answer Jesus gave when asked in John 9 about the man born blind.

> *Jesus answered, "It was not that this man sinned, or his parents, but that the works of God might be displayed in him."*
> John 9:3, ESV

Now, I was to use all the tears that led to our daughter to manifest God's power to others. When we share our stories, it is so others may see God: His power, His character, and His salvation. We get to become a tangible picture of who God is. Let us not be so quick to rush through a trial that we avoid the full work of sanctification. People need to see the change in us so they may see God all the more clearly, and we need to persevere under trial so we may be able to tell of the goodness of God.

Contrary to what is easy to believe, we must not forget that God is for us. He is at work even if we cannot see it. He is with us. He is building us into who we were always created to be. He is equipping us to play the long game with heaven in mind. Friend, He is making sure that the trials and suffering we experience are not in vain. While we will never be completely sanctified in this life, He is making sure we are ready for eternity with Him.

part III: triumph

> "Somehow you'll escape
> all that waiting and staying.
> You'll find the bright places
> where Boom Bands are playing.
>
> With banner flip-flapping,
> once more you'll ride high!
> Ready for anything under the sky.
> Ready because you're that kind of a guy!"

the struggle is real

triumph

a note on triumph

Triumph won't always look like we think it should, but part of the victory comes in admitting the struggle. Part of the reason we try to cover our struggle and take it on alone is that we value the wrong things. We think strength is independence and a victory obvious to everyone. But, we have no idea what true strength is.

In the book of Daniel, we are exposed to the story of four young men who have been captured from the tribe of Judah: Daniel, Hananiah, Mishael, and Azariah. These young men came from the royal tribe and could have easily fought their capture, yet they did not. Instead, they were taken to a place where their familiar, holy teaching was stripped and disregarded, and their identities that declared them of the tribe of Judah were disregarded. Daniel became Belteshazzar, Hananiah became Shadrach, Mishael took the name Meshach, and Azariah was given Abednego. Yet, these young men still submitted to their captors.

Let's just pause for a moment. These names they were given robbed them of the identity they had known for their entire lives; it stripped them of being able to identify with the royal tribe of Judah—the same one the Messiah was to be a part of. Now, if this had been me, those would have been fightin' words. Let's not forget, they were also asked to renounce all the familiar, holy teaching so that they might serve a king who was, to say the least, egotistical. They were uprooted, torn from their families, captured by an enemy, yet they still didn't fight back.

It seems those young men just sat back and accepted defeat. But just as we start to think that, we see Daniel take a stand. These young men were asked to violate God's law by eating food that was unclean, and Daniel began to buck those imprisoning him and the others. Certainly, they would not simply accept this defeat. As God granted them favor, He also gave the victory of eating clean food.

However, they were still held captive in a pagan land that continued to ask them to violate God's law.

When the declaration was made by King Nebuchadnezzar that his people must worship the golden image he had made, Shadrach, Meshach, and Abednego refused to bow down, even though they knew it might very well cost them their lives.

Naturally, this stand for God angered the egotistical, pagan king, and he sought to kill them by throwing them into the fiery furnace, but not before mocking the God they served. Things looked bleak. Again, these young men did not fight back. They simply stepped into the furnace, telling King Nebuchadnezzar, "If this be so, our God who we serve is able to deliver us from the burning fiery furnace, and he will deliver us out of your hand, O king. But if not, be it known to you, O king, that we will not serve your gods or worship the golden image that you have set up" (Daniel 3:17-18, ESV).

Ummmm…excuse me?! These guys were getting ready to meet their death, yet they still remained strong in their resolve not to worship anyone but God. They knew God could rescue them, and they were probably hoping He would. After all, that would be a triumph and bring great glory to God. But they continued on to say they realized victory might not look like they'd envisioned.

In the same way, God can rescue us and give us tangible victories at any point in our trials, but if not, He is still a good, victorious God, and by association, we are victorious. We share in His victory just as we do His suffering because we are His children.

Victory means that regardless of the outcome, God is glorified because triumph comes when we stand firm in the truth of who He is.

the struggle is real

chapter 10: triumph surviving

the struggle is real

chapter 10: triumph surviving

When I was a freshman in high school, both of my parents became self-employed when they bought a business from a friend at church. This seemed like a good option because it would give them more free time to come to my events, it would get my mom out of a job she felt stuck in, and it would allow her to help my dad with his other business. There were many talks with attorneys to be sure expectations were clear, but it was mostly just a formality. After all, this was a friend from church whom everyone loved.

It was July when the contract was finally signed, and we all jumped in with both feet, excited for a new adventure that would allow us not only more time but more income (Full transparency: I was a bit less than excited. We had just bought a portable toilet company). We hardly had time to think because it was summer—the busy season. We were up before dawn most days, working through the sweltering heat and making sure construction sites, parades, holiday parties, and other events had what they needed to accommodate their guests. Often, we wouldn't be in bed until after dark. Trying to learn the ropes in the midst of a busy season put us in survival mode. We were working hard, and we knew that we would see the benefits soon.

the struggle is real

As summer drifted away without a vacation, and the days got shorter, we continued with the long hours. The friendship we had with the seller seemed to be different, but we figured it was because we were trying to separate business and pleasure. However, everything was business. When the next busy season rolled around a year later, we were still in survival mode.

Yes, something felt off. Surely it shouldn't be this way always. We kept pushing, making a few adjustments here and there as time would allow, but we kept being run dry. Instead of being able to enjoy free time and financial gain, we were more tied down than ever. We were simply trying to keep our heads above water. So, when a call came in, we would delay a vacation or a free night to have a chance at earning a buck or two, regardless of how badly the rest was needed.

Our bills were paid, we met some interesting people, saw some awesome places, and heard stories, but by the beginning of my junior year, I realized I wanted to eat dinner without talking about a toilet. I wanted to feel like we were not simply surviving; I wanted to see my family thrive. The friendship that started it all had dissolved because the pursuit of money above all else made it apparent we were simply a means to an end. Our relationships with each other were fine, for the most part, but we needed to reconnect over something that wasn't just business. We needed to get out of the cycle of just getting by. I could tell my parents were worn out: work, sleep, eat, work, sleep, eat, work, sleep, eat. I, at least, could escape to school.

Along the way, we acquired a wooden outhouse that became a sort of symbol for us. When we did advertisements in parades, we pulled it on a trailer. It was unique and cute, certainly catching people's attention. When not rolling through a parade, it sat in the front corner of the lot that served as the hub for business and was thought about very little. One day, we looked up and noticed it was leaning a bit to one side and had become weathered by the elements. As we drove out of the lot, hooked up for a delivery, I made a quip regarding how it looked is how we all felt. Smirking in agreement, we drove off.

As yet another summer approached, we carved out time to celebrate my high school graduation and the advent of my college career-my pursuit of being a first-generation college graduate. In those moments, we realized that while we were so far gone into survival mode, it had been a solid four years since we stepped out into any sort of semblance of thriving. We were disenchanted with our existence, despite the fact we had created a good life: we had little connection with friends, we didn't have time to enjoy things, we were constantly moving from one thing to the next, with no room to process.

In my mind, the solution was easy: walk away. Give the business back, or sell it. Nothing was worth this. These feelings were no secret to my parents, the little outhouse in the corner of the lot reflecting the same sentiment.

Behind the scenes, my parents were feeling the same way, but they kept on pushing forward looking for the light, for hope, and for a way to thrive. Adjustments continued to be made to free up time while making the most of the income, but it seemed like no matter what they did, the light never even flickered.

the struggle is real

I started to get a hint of the desire to close up shop when I suggested getting rid of the dilapidated outhouse that was no longer serving a purpose. We couldn't even pull it in the parade of Christmas lights that year because there was no way it would make it down the road without flying apart. My mom, run ragged, found a burst of energy to utter, "We can't. Until it falls down, we can't quit." As it turned out, the outhouse served as a beacon of hope for her. In the next few months, I found myself praying for that dumb little outhouse to implode on itself, but it seemed to keep standing.

Finally, at the end of September, during my sophomore year of college, I watched the outhouse lose a board, and that was the final straw. As the missing board let light into the darkened outhouse, light began to flood into our hearts; maybe we could finally get out of survival mode and move back into the land of the living. A few days later, my parents delivered the final portable toilet, truck, and trailer to the man we once thought of as a friend. They got in the car, relieved, and drove away without ever looking back.

"The outhouse finally fell down," my mom told me when I got home that day. To say I was excited might be the understatement of the century, but we finally were able to bask in the light again. No more talk of toilets at the table. No more endless work days. No more struggling. No more forced smiles in an effort to appear present and okay. Even as we nursed our scars—dealing with the consequences financially, emotionally, relationally, and even physically—there was light. We could begin the long road to thriving once again, as it was lit by the light of hope.

In those years, as we fought for every step between stress and sleep, it became apparent that when we are in the trenches of battle it is hard, if not impossible, to see the light at the end of it. We may be whispering in our souls, "If I can just make it through this…" God knows it feels that way.

Friend, there is no shame in being bloodied and bruised when coming out of a trial. As a matter of fact, when people see those scars, that is what grants us the permission to share where we've been and how God has been faithful. But just as you're clawing your way out of that pit, that isn't your focus. Your focus is simply surviving. In that moment, survival is enough.

In the months and years following trials, it is likely we revisit those dark days. We still try to reconcile to ourselves where we went wrong, what led us into that battle, or maybe if we will ever be okay again. We still have questions for God, but we are careful not to dwell there too long, lest we venture back to the bottom of that pit.

But in the light of reprieve, we are simply thankful we survived. Sure, the struggle might have just been a bad day spent yelling at the kids, the water heater breaking, the line for pick up at school had a terrible traffic jam, or praying the kids would just fall asleep already! It might have been walking through the death of a loved one, relocating to a new job in a new town, or a divorce. The truth remains; our one goal was to make it through.

We still find ourselves asking things like, "Why me?" or "What did I do?" or "What am I supposed to get out of this?" While those questions are valid and understandable to ask, they reflect the skewed perspective we have when we face trials. The center of each of those questions is *me*. The fact of the matter is that we may never know why we experience these trials, and we struggle with that concept. As a general rule, we are me-focused rather than He-focused. Throw in battling through a trial, and the misplaced focus is amplified.

It is easy to look around at the current state of the world, take stock, and only see the terrible. It's easy to believe we are doomed. And that may be true if it weren't for Christ. It is because of Christ's death on the cross and His resurrection three days later that we are not sentenced to doom. Instead, we have victory. Jesus provides encouragement as He says, "I have said these things to you, that in me you may have peace. In the world you will have tribulation. But take heart; I have overcome the world" (John 16:33, ESV).

Don't miss this promise, friend! Jesus tells us the reason He gave us these words is so that they are a source of peace. Why? Because we will face difficulties. We will absolutely come face to face with millions of things we are not able to handle. Instead of leaving us to sulk in our misery, Jesus reminds us that we can be encouraged because He has overcome the world. That is to say that none of the perils of this world have anything on us if we are in Christ. He wins! We win!

To the enemy, those are fighting words. Because the enemy knows we are at war, he takes full advantage of the fact we live in a broken and fallen world. He uses every conniving tactic he can think of to pull our focus off Christ and onto ourselves. He wants nothing more than to make us think we are alone in our despair and desperation. He desires for us to be confused, hurt, isolated, and busy. He twists the truth. He does absolutely everything he can to make us forget the promise that packs his death blow.

Most of the habits we find ourselves practicing are to prevent the attacks of the enemy. We think that if we can just pay close enough attention, make the right choices, and be kind to all the people we meet, then we will be spared the grueling task of working through trials. We work to protect ourselves and those we love. It seems that even though we know trials are inevitable, maybe these protocols we set in place will lessen the blow or spare us from at least a few. While that's not all bad, this idea of protection can easily turn into an idol that we pursue more than trusting God. We are guaranteed trials, and while we can't control the trials themselves, we can control our response to them. Suffering requires our cooperation.

While God saves us, we work in tandem with Him through our process of sanctification, which inevitably includes suffering. The cooperation required of us is that we seek out our Savior. In the midst of our trials, we look to our Savior so we may see a glimmer of hope in the darkness. We look to Him for our help. All the while, He is at work on our behalf and within us. He goes before us, to make the places that are hard for us to navigate, a bit more manageable. He works within us to grow us, so we may be abounding in the fruits of the Spirit. He is getting a hold of our hearts and molding our perspective.

You see, our perspective changes everything. When we understand that our only job is to trust God, it is easier to fight through every inch of trial. This in no way diminishes those trials that seem to break us. We cannot simply say that a relationship with Jesus and understanding of who He is will be the cure for all our suffering. Instead, He is the source of all things that help shift our perspective. Our perspective shift may come in the form of therapy. It may be an antidepressant. It may be the care of a group of doctors responsible for helping you work through mental health issues or a possible medical condition, whether chronic or acute. It may simply be a friend you can call at three o'clock in the morning when you wake up and can't go back to sleep. Maybe it's a song that comes on the radio as you are driving. These are all resources to which our Savior gives us access.

We operate with the understanding that God gave friends and professionals the ability to care for us, help us, and champion us. God is the one who places people where He needs them in the exact right moment so we may see Him. Peter says, "Therefore, let those who suffer according to God's will entrust their souls to a faithful Creator while doing good" (1 Peter 4:19, ESV). God never intended that we suffer alone, and even though it may feel like it at times, He is not ignorant of our suffering. In fact, had the Lord not allowed it, we would not experience it. The intent is that we first lean on Him, seek Him out, and then follow His direction. That direction may be to a doctor or to a quiet place to meet with Him. We are safe to follow that direction, wherever it leads because our God is trustworthy.

When we take God at His word, trusting Him to lead us through trials, not only are we able to build a deeper relationship with Him, but we are able to see His heart a bit better. In the moments that are crushing, our desperation drives us to the refuge of Christ. There, we build the muscles it takes to think with the mind of Christ, as He becomes our source of joy, despite the chaos around us.

Delight yourself in the Lord, and he will give you the desires of your heart. Commit your way to the Lord; trust in him, and he will act.
Psalm 37:4-5, ESV

When we know God intimately and seek His heart in all things, our desires become His desires. This is not to say we control His desires. Rather, He has transformed our hearts and our lives to look more like His. The Lord always desires for us what is in our best interest, and when we aren't staying connected to Him, our hearts tend to run contradictory to His. To prevent this, He calls us to delight in Him because He is enough. Not only that, He tells us the way we are able to delight in Him is through commitment. Sometimes, we have to boss our emotions around so we can see clearly. When we trust God, we have the privilege of seeing Him move mountains we didn't even know needed moving.

But that's just like our God. He allows us to see trials, and as hard as they may seem, He grants us grace to walk through them. He doesn't leave us to do this alone because God knows we would fail miserably in that case. Instead, He walks with us, protecting us because He is for us. Jude 29 tells us that God is able to "keep" us in order that we may be presented blameless when we find ourselves in His presence (ESV). We are never so far gone that we are out of His reach; we are never out of the range of His protection. While the protection He provides may look different than our earthly minds are accustomed to understanding, we must hold on to the truth that He is guarding us.

If we are to remain in Christ in the midst of trials, when God seems so far away, we must press into Him and trust Him to be our refuge. Otherwise, we won't survive the trials. We can know all of the truths of suffering from the reasons to the truths that are capable of combating the lies of the enemy, but if we fail to apply them, we stand no chance of being victorious. We couldn't even scrape by with simply surviving a trial, apart from the power of God. We must act on what we believe, and when it's hard to believe, we must act on the truth. This will push us to the heart of the Lord.

chapter 11: here for the fight

the struggle is real

chapter 11: here for the fight

In our weakness, the enemy is on the prowl for our vulnerabilities, and we must arm ourselves unless we want the enemy to overtake us. Fortunately, we already have every weapon we need to fight that deceitful devil. This is a good thing because we couldn't wage this war with supplies found on earth. Instead, we must fight with the spiritual weapons found in God alone.

> *Put on the whole armor of God, that you may be able to stand against the schemes of the devil. For we do not wrestle against flesh and blood, but against the rulers, against the authorities, against the cosmic powers over this present darkness, against the spiritual forces of evil in the heavenly places. Therefore take up the whole armor of God, that you may be able to withstand in the evil day, and having done all, to stand firm. Stand therefore, having fastened on the belt of truth, and having put on the breastplate of righteousness, and, as shoes for your feet, having put on the readiness given by the gospel of peace. In all circumstances take up the shield of faith, with which you can extinguish all the flaming darts of the evil one; and take the helmet of salvation, and the sword of the Spirit, which is the word of God.*
> Ephesians 6:11-18, ESV

We have a fully equipped suit of armor that allows us to withstand the attacks of the enemy. This armor, as Priscilla Shirer points out in her Bible study, *The Armor of God*, is the same armor the Lord Himself uses. If we reach all the way back to Isaiah 59:17, we are able to see this as we are told that God equipped Himself as the fighter He desires us to be when He "put on righteousness as a breastplate, and a helmet of salvation" (ESV). Do you know what that tells me? If I equip myself with the tools He has given me, I can put up a pretty darn good fight against the enemy. Not only that, but because of Him, those weapons will allow me to be victorious, no matter how bruised and bloodied I may be when I emerge from the battle.

Truth be told, the only way we can fight our real enemy, the one that led the charge to the Fall, is to utilize the weapons of spiritual warfare. The Word makes it very clear in 2 Corinthians 10:4-5 that these weapons are created specifically for divine warfare and have the ability to destroy strongholds. That's good news, y'all! The Lord gives us the tools we need to battle things that have previously paralyzed and held us captive for so long, whether it be sin, trauma, or brokenness. And while God may choose not to take ailments away or heal them in a way our earthly minds can come up with, He is still giving us His victory. This means that because of Him, we are not bound to strongholds for eternity; they will be destroyed. When we remember this in the trenches of trial, our victory is not far behind. However, we must remember the victory of Christ is not the same as the victory of this world.

Can I just level with you for a quick minute?

I don't want you to read this and think, "I mean, that sounds great, but the truth is, I can't see that right now." Or maybe you're thinking instead, "Listen; I've prayed. I've fasted.

I've asked all the questions. I've been faithful, but God hasn't delivered me from any of my (name your stronghold that doesn't go away here)." I get it. At times, I've been in pits so dark I never thought I would see light again. I have wished numerous times things could "just go back to the way they were before." I still desperately yearn not to be consumed by guilt and thoughts of what I used to be, how I have cursed God, how I have doubted my salvation. There are so many things I wish I could change, whether regret or being subject to hurt, trauma, and brokenness. Sister, I wish I could change the tragedies for you too, but I don't have that power. Only our Savior does. And if we believe that with our whole hearts, living in light of that truth brings us to the sober reality that God may not heal us or destroy strongholds in the way we see fit. That doesn't mean He has failed us. As a matter of fact, He can't fail us. It's not in His nature.

The Bible puts it this way: "So death is at work in us, but life in you. Since we have the same spirit of faith according to what has been written, 'I believed, and so I spoke,' we also believe, and so we also speak…" (2 Corinthians 4:12-13, ESV). Unfortunately, all we know on this side of heaven is the grip of death. We are constantly battling, fighting, and striving for what it means to have LIFE. The products of the Fall: sin, brokenness, trauma, hurt, anger, and all the other miseries that plague us can easily wear mere mortals down. But because we have life in Christ, we get to see—even in the midst of survival mode—a glimmer of victory. With that glimmer of victory, we get to choose to take God at His word, living as David did, even in the midst of struggles, and act on who we believe God to be as well as that which we believe God is capable of doing.

Let's not fall victim to the lies the enemy would have us believe at our most vulnerable moments when we're coming out of trial bruised and bloodied. Instead, let us cling to the Word. The truth of God's Word isn't meant to dismiss our hurt. It isn't intended to push aside the wounds and make us move forward as though nothing happened. The Word of God is meant to minister to us. It's a beacon, a life raft, and hope when the Light is hard to see.

Put simply, the key to making it to triumph mode, even if it is simply surviving, is taking God at His Word.

chapter 12: thriving after the fight

the struggle is real

chapter 12: thriving after the fight

I sat across the table from my sweet friend Jill and her husband, Matt. The coffee shop was quiet, the coffee steaming. "If you're depressed, it's okay to talk to a doctor. There is no shame in taking a pill. My depression kicked in after I had my son, and this pill has been helpful." I tried not to react, but I admittedly sat in stunned silence.

This woman I so admired, this woman who might be the most joy-filled person I knew, just admitted to me out of the clear blue sky, that she was taking antidepressants…and had been longer than I imagined. I also wondered where the statement came from since I had yet to tell her of all the internal wars I had been waging.

To this point, my husband had found me sitting on our bed, audibly sobbing, more times in the last six months than I may have ever cried in my whole life. He would console me as we fell asleep at night, and I would wake up with a smile plastered on my face and head to work each day. We went to all the fun small-town events that ring in each season. You know, the ones where everyone takes the perfect pictures worthy of being published in a magazine. We went to football games and volleyball games—things I used to love. I went to a conference with my mom at a girl's weekend for the first time ever in an effort to find joy. But because I was battling all of the lies I'd let the enemy place into the core of my being, they all felt empty. All the things that used to bring joy all felt…fake.

I hated these feelings because they weren't the me I knew. I wrestled with the thought that I was either crazy or depressed, but I spoke to no one other than my mom and husband about it. I talked myself out of the possibility that I could be struggling with suicidal thoughts because that had never been me, and there had been nothing to set that off in me. I figured the fewer people that knew I might be face to face with the monster that could potentially cause me to think about suicide, the less likely it was I actually had depression. So, Jill certainly didn't know.

I stared at her blankly, waiting for her to impart more wisdom. She continued, "These things don't change how loved you are or who you are." I felt protest rising inside me, but I suppressed it. When we left the coffee shop that day, my brain was spinning. I allowed myself to protest in the car:

But THAT isn't who I am.
I KNOW I am loved, but I don't feel loved.
Where is God? Why can't I feel Him? Is it because I've lost my salvation?
There is no way I currently am or have ever actually been depressed. Why would she even say that? Do I look like I'm in bad shape like I'm not okay?

As we walked in the door to our new home, a symbol of a fresh start to me, my husband, who had made himself like a fly on the wall during this conversation, asked, "Have you told her any of what we've been dealing with the last six months?"

"No."

He smirked. He knew what had just happened was only because of God. Then, he said the thing I never wanted him to say. "I think you have been battling depression." Well, shoot. If he just said it, it must be true.

In that moment, I was the most devastated, yet freed, I might have ever been. Because he was my safe place, I couldn't contain my protests any longer. As is his nature, he listened calmly with understanding.

"Keagan, rest in what you KNOW. Our feelings are not always the truth, and sometimes, they aren't that great at giving any sort of accurate information. Be sure those feelings you're choosing to listen to are rooted in truth. And while this isn't who you've known yourself to be, God is constantly growing us into who He needs us to be for His glory, even if it isn't what we had pictured."

Finally, I knew what was wrong. For months, I had simply existed, barely in survival mode, in a pit of darkness. I couldn't ever seem to get my head above water, and I certainly didn't believe what I knew could possibly be true. The walls of my pit were painted with sunshine and laughter, but they were empty of actual life. I had an explanation for why nothing ever felt exactly as I was used to it feeling and why I so desperately longed for "the way things were before," even though it seemed—on the outside—like nothing had changed. I knew there were ways to fix this persistent problem, but I didn't really want that label—who does?

the struggle is real

This revelation gave me the tenacity to start clawing my way out of the pit where I could finally see with some clarity all that God had been teaching me. Maybe I didn't have to just struggle through each day, hoping to survive. Maybe I could really learn to thrive while I struggle.

In the middle of the darkness, we gasp for air. We sulk in the silence, wondering if we will ever be normal again. Survival is all we can imagine. There is no laughter. There are few smiles. Anything we do feels void of significance. We can't seem to bring ourselves to hope for a day where we truly, deeply laugh, smile with sincerity, or feel anything again. When we're just trying to survive, everything seems empty.

It's okay to be there. It's understandable to feel these things. It's normal to wonder if things could ever be—at the very least—okay again.

Because of Jesus, we know that there is life, not only past the pain but in the midst of it as well. It's true we may be in a place that is dark and hopeless; there are seasons like that.

Remember Shadrach, Meshach, and Abednego? After some time in the fire, the king noticed a fourth man in the fire, and all were unbound, walking around, and unharmed. Here's the thing: Jehovah Roi—God our Protector—gets down in the furnace with us and walks with us in the midst of trial. Because of this, we are able to exist simultaneously in the pit of despair as well as in the safety of our Protector. This allows us to thrive in the middle of our struggles.

Make no mistake: regardless of what we know, trials and struggles are painful. There is no amount of knowledge that can take that away. Instead, that knowledge allows us to prepare for the fact that we will experience this hurt. We can be intentional with how we choose to respond to our struggles each and every day and to how we choose to apply all of these principles the Bible gives us as a guide. Our intentionality doesn't take away the hurt, but it does allow us to see God in the middle of it. It has the power to keep us out of (or pull us away from) the grips of simply surviving.

Here's the deal. When we learn to struggle well, it is easier to keep the hope of God at the forefront of our minds, no matter how bleak the situation may seem. Struggling well doesn't mean we don't see darkness, nor does it mean we will never enter survival mode again. Instead, it means that we choose to focus on Christ and rest in Him entirely. When we struggle, we go into a struggle default mode, if you will, and if we don't choose to make running to Christ our first choice, then we only seek Him in our most desperate moments.

When the hope of God is our focus, it is easy to remember suffering is not eternal, if we are in Christ. It is a plague we are only subject to in this lifetime. While the struggles are only on this side of heaven, the work done in us is not. The goal of God allowing us to experience these things is twofold: for His glory and for our good. He is making us more like Him in order to prepare us for eternity.

In his exploration of suffering, Trent Butler puts it this way: "Suffering gives rise to hope." Now, that may seem a bit counterintuitive, but the Word supports this idea in Romans 12:12 saying, "Rejoice in hope, be patient in tribulation, be constant in prayer" (ESV). Why would hope and tribulation be mentioned together? Obviously, there is some link between the two. You see, when we have hope, it allows us to rejoice, no matter the circumstance. However, because we know that when we have hope in bleak situations we can grow weary, we must keep in mind that our trials require patience. This is because they either require long-suffering or because they are constant. This is growing in us a steadfast hope in Christ (1 Thessalonians 1:3). The only way to accomplish both is the last command of that verse: prayer. If we try by our sheer willpower to have hope and to be patient in the midst of all our junk, we will not succeed. Instead, we will fall flat on our faces. We must connect with our source of hope as well as the One who is able to walk through trials with us and empower us.

Admittedly, it is hard to know at times that God is walking with us, no matter how many times we've seen it be true before. When I finally gave my season of depression a name, I was far enough removed to know and remember the truth that God was even in the midst of that. But in those dark months...

I felt alone. Crazy. Neglected. Unseen. Hopeless.

Would anything ever be right and good again? Would I ever know happiness? Why couldn't things just be like they were before *gestures wildly at the world* this?

I saw my husband desperately trying to figure out how to walk with me lovingly through that season, but I remember pacing the driveway wondering where God had disappeared to. I cried out to Him under the warmth of the sun and the coolness of the spring breeze—I probably seemed like a crazy person to the neighbors peering out their windows or those creeping down the street in their vehicles.

"God? Where are you? Why can't I feel you? Why can't I

see you? Why do I feel so crazy? We need you here. I need you here." The tears were hot against my face as I thought about how tired I was of feeling sad, neglected, lost, and hopeless.

As humans, we are prone to think that at some point He is going to forget us and neglect us, but we forget that's not in His nature; it's in ours. He is not us, but He knows us more intimately than we can ever dream of knowing each other. For this reason, He gives us people to act as a picture of Him as we trudge through our struggles each day. He knows we need to know we are not alone, especially in our weakest moments or our darkest places.

Over and over, we feel the weight of our struggles. At times, this weight can feel crushing, but often it's because we are trying to bear the burden on our own. It was never meant to be that way. Sister, we were created for community. The Triune God Himself set this example for us. Not only that but repeatedly throughout scripture we see this example set as God calls His people to unity in Philippians 2:2. In 1 Peter 5:9, we are reminded that in our suffering, we are not alone because there is a "brotherhood" around the world that has experienced the same trials (ESV). In Galatians 6:2, we are commanded to bear the burdens of each other. When the weight of the world is piled on your shoulders, and it all gets to be too much, it is okay, even wise, to admit you cannot do it on your own. You need people to come alongside you and champion you, fight for you, pray with you, and pray for you when you don't have the words.

The fact is, we are better together.

Two are better than one, because they have a good reward

for their toil. For if they fall, one will lift up his fellow. But woe to him who is alone when he falls and has not another to lift him up! Again, if two lie together, they keep warm, but how can one keep warm alone? And though a man might prevail against one who is alone, two will withstand him – a threefold cord is not quickly broken.
Ecclesiastes 4:9-12, ESV

You may have heard this passage at weddings, but it is just as effective as it points to the power of community. When things get rough, we are to hold each other accountable, act as a team, and point each other back to Christ. We aren't supposed to fight our battles alone. We have our hope in Christ, the full armor of God, and a community of believers to remind us of the Light that will guide us out of our mess.

Because of this, the enemy loves nothing more than to either isolate us or make us feel isolated. When nobody is around to remind us of truth, and when God seems so far away, it is easy for us to succumb to the lies of the enemy because those lies begin to sound like truth. The enemy loves to take something that sounds like truth and make us believe it actually is truth. When we are in the midst of struggling, it can be difficult to tell the difference. If we are to thrive in the midst of trial, we cannot allow that to happen.

We need to arm ourselves with the belt of truth as well as a community of people who are constantly pointing us back to the truth. Our community is critical. Truth be told, I learned the hard way that asking for help or prayers doesn't make you weak. Instead, it shows you know you cannot do this alone.

I held on to my pride and kept my struggles close to the

vest. The only ones aware of the depth of my pain were my mom and my husband; there may have been two other close friends who knew I wasn't completely okay. I was afraid to be vulnerable in this way. After all, I'm the friend that rallies you, gathers a community to walk through the storm with you, and starts the prayer chain. I thought if that was my role, I could not be the one in need of those things. But that's another lie of the enemy. We all get a turn at the table to be a mess, and we all get a turn to rally troops. You were never meant to do this on your own. That's part of why God built us for community.

Since we all get a turn to rally the troops, we must recognize that as believers, we need to be quick to come alongside those in our community, being willing to walk through the fire with those around us that are suffering.

We need each other to move ahead, and we need far more than tired old phrases. In times when life becomes unmanageable, we need to be willing to walk alongside one another. When we do this, we put flesh and bone on the person of Jesus...When we are willing to sit in the pain, to walk with one another when life's path is difficult and to shoulder one another's burdens when they are too heavy, we become an embodied promise. We become living proof that while life can sometimes be too much, through the goodness of our loving of God displayed within us, we can move forward together.

The early church is a perfect example of this. Not only did they set aside their selfish desires in humility, but they gave of themselves. These Christians did not let a person in their community be in need of anything because those who had the resources to help their fellow community members did (Acts

4:32-37). The early church set the precedent that brothers and sisters were not to face their battles alone, whether there be a financial issue or a spiritual one. Helping wasn't a question, and there was no hesitation. They just did because they knew that's what they were called to do. Giving of ourselves and showing compassion to others is what it means to be the hands and feet of Jesus. This is part of how God carries us through our daily struggles and our darkest suffering.

Dear one,

Let us not be disillusioned to think we will always thrive in suffering. Sometimes, we will not be able to put one foot in front of the other, much less look up into the face of God. Sometimes, it has to be enough to simply survive. Yet, because God is near to the broken-hearted, we can suffer well (Psalm 34:18-19). He gets on our level to meet us where we are, even to the point of carrying us through the fire. He is in the midst of it all with us, never failing us. Our job is to hold tightly to Him and boldly step forward as He lights the way. We must not shrink back—we cannot shrink back—so that even when our knees are wobbly and our face tear-stained, others may see Him and know Him.

"So…
be your name Buxbaum or Bixby or Bray
or Mordecai Ali Van Allen O'Shea,
you're off to Great Places!
Today is your day!
Your mountain is waiting.
So…get on your way!"

the struggle is real

bibliography

Butler, Trent C. "Entry for Suffering". Holman Bible Dictionary. Accessed February 24, 2022. https://www.studylight.org/dictionaries/eng/hbd/s/suffering.html.

Clarke, Adam. "Commentary on Galatians 6." The Adam Clarke Commentary. Accessed February 23, 2020. https://www.studylight.org/commentaries/eng/acc/galatians-6.html.

Constable, Thomas. "Commentary on Job 1." Expository Notes of Dr. Thomas Constable vol. III. Accessed February 24, 2022. https://www.studylight.org/commentaries/eng/dcc/job-1.html.

Fleming, Don. Entry for 'Suffering'. Bridgeway Bible Dictionary. Accessed February 24, 2022. https://www.studylight.org/dictionaries/eng/bbd/s/suffering.html.

Grudem, Wayne. "Sanctification." In Systematic Theology: An Introduction to Biblical Doctrine. Grand Rapids, MI: Zondervan, 1994.

Henry, Matthew. "The Safety of Those Who Have God for Their Refuge (91:1-8)." In Matthew Henry's Concise

Commentary of the Whole Bible. Nashville, TN: Thomas Nelson, 2003.

Keathley, J. Hampton. "Why Christians Suffer." Bible.org. Accessed February 24, 2022. https://bible.org/article/why-christians-suffer.

Merriam-Webster.com Dictionary. "Promise." Accessed June 30, 2020, https://www.merriam-webster.com/dictionary/promise.

National Aeronautics and Space Administration. "Newton's Laws of Motion." Glenn Research Center, edited by Peter Santana Rodriguez, May 5, 2015. https://www1.grc.nasa.gov/beginners-guide-to-aeronautics/newtons-laws-of-motion/.

Relevant Magazine Staff. "Yes, God Will Give You More Than You Can Handle." Relevant Magazine, July 21, 2020. www.relevantmagazine.com/culture/yes-god-will-give-you-more-than-you-can-handle/.

Ross, Allen P., Shepard, Jerry E., and Schwab, George M. "Zeal, without knowledge (19:2)." In The Expositor's Bible Commentary Revised Edition: Proverbs, Ecclesiastes, Song of Songs, edited by Tremper Longman III and David E. Garland. Grand Rapids, MI: Zondervan, 2012.

Suess, Dr. Oh, The Places You'll Go. New York, NY: Random House Children's Books, 1986.

Smick, Elmer B. "Job 1." In The Expositor's Bible Commentary, Volume 4: 1&2 Kings, 1&2 Chronicles, Ezra, Nehemiah, Esther, Job, edited by Frank Gaebelein. Grand

Rapids, MI: Zondervan, 1988.

Sutcliffe, Joseph. "Commentary on Psalms 91:4." Sutcliffe's Commentary on the Old and New Testaments. Accessed February 24, 2022. https://www.studylight.org/commentaries/jsc/psalms-91.html.

Thayer and Smith. "Greek Lexicon entry for Dokimazo." The NAS New Testament Greek Lexicon. 1999.

the struggle is real

about the author

Keagan Hayden is a wife, mom, and Christian women's communicator. With a Bachelors in Communication Education, she is a former teacher and cheer coach in a tiny town in Texas where she lives with her husband Levi and two children. She is on a mission to see women set free as they discover the truth about their identity in Christ. She's also still trying to figure out how to create a balanced diet of chocolate, spaghetti, and Dr. Pepper.

You can follow Keagan on social media at facebook.com/keagankhayden, instagram.com/keagankhayden, and twitter.com/keagankayetexas. Sign up for her newsletter or learn more on her website at www.keagankhayden.com

www.ingramcontent.com/pod-product-compliance
Lightning Source LLC
Chambersburg PA
CBHW030329100526
44592CB00010B/634